Exploring the Spectrum

A Compass for Understanding Gender Diversity

Ph.D. TONY SMITH

Exploring the Spectrum

Ph.D. Tony Smith

Exploring the Spectrum

Table of Content

Exploring the Spectrum

Ph.D. Tony Smith

Book Introduction

In the tapestry of human experience, the concept of gender has long been regarded as a binary construct, neatly divided into the categories of male and female. However, as our understanding of human diversity continues to evolve, it has become increasingly clear that gender exists on a spectrum, encompassing a rich and nuanced array of identities, expressions, and lived experiences.

This book serves as a comprehensive guide to navigating the intricate landscape of gender diversity, providing a compassionate and inclusive perspective that challenges long-held assumptions and invites us to embrace the fullness of human experience. Through personal narratives, scholarly insights, and practical strategies, we embark on a journey that expands our understanding of gender, celebrates diversity, and empowers individuals to live authentically and freely.

The journey begins by examining the historical and cultural underpinnings of the gender binary, exploring how societal norms and expectations have shaped our perceptions of gender. We delve into the lived experiences of individuals whose identities transcend the traditional binary, highlighting their stories of resilience, self-discovery, and the pursuit of acceptance. By amplifying these voices, we gain a deeper appreciation for the multifaceted nature of gender and the importance of creating inclusive spaces where all individuals can thrive.

Exploring the Spectrum

Throughout the chapters, we unpack the complexities of language and terminology, recognizing the power of words to validate or marginalize individuals. We explore the legal and policy frameworks that protect the rights of individuals across the gender spectrum, advocating for equal access, dignity, and representation. Additionally, we examine the unique health considerations and support systems essential for the well-being of transgender and gender-nonconforming individuals.

The book delves into the nuances of building and fostering communities that embrace gender diversity, fostering a sense of belonging and acceptance. We navigate the intricacies of relationships and intimacy, offering insights and guidance for individuals navigating their identities and expressions. Furthermore, we explore the challenges and opportunities of raising children in a gender-expansive society, equipping parents and caregivers with the tools to nurture and support their children's authentic selves.

In the realms of work and professional endeavors, we shed light on the importance of fostering inclusive and affirming environments, where individuals of all gender identities and expressions can thrive and contribute their talents without fear of discrimination or bias. We also confront the insidious nature of unconscious biases and societal assumptions, providing strategies for self-reflection, education, and personal growth.

Recognizing the invaluable role of allies in the journey towards gender inclusivity, we explore the principles and practices of effective allyship. We offer guidance on how to actively support, advocate for, and uplift individuals across the gender spectrum, fostering a culture of empathy, respect, and solidarity.

Ph.D. Tony Smith

As we venture into the artistic realms, we celebrate the myriad ways in which gender identity and expression intersect with creativity, showcasing the powerful narratives and perspectives that emerge through various art forms. We also delve into the interplay between gender diversity and spirituality, exploring how different religious and philosophical traditions have grappled with and embraced gender diversity throughout history.

Furthermore, we examine the intersection of gender and politics, highlighting the voices and activism of individuals who have fought tirelessly for equality, representation, and social change. We explore the ongoing battles for legal protections, access to healthcare, and the dismantling of systemic barriers that marginalize and oppress individuals based on their gender identities and expressions.

Ultimately, this book invites us to envision a future where gender diversity is celebrated, respected, and embraced as a fundamental aspect of the human experience. We explore the potential for societal transformation, where individuals are free to express their authentic selves without fear or judgment, and where diversity is recognized as a source of strength, enrichment, and personal fulfillment.

Throughout these pages, we weave together personal narratives, scholarly insights, and practical strategies, creating a tapestry that celebrates the beauty and resilience of the human spirit. This book serves as a catalyst for understanding, empathy, and action, inspiring us to embrace the full spectrum of gender identity and expression, and to create a more just, inclusive, and compassionate world for all.

Exploring the Spectrum

Chapter 1

From Binary to Spectrum: Expanding Our View of Gender

Exploring the Spectrum

Understanding the Gender Binary and Why We Must Move Beyond It

For most of modern history, we have viewed gender as a strict male-female binary, with nothing in between. This binary categorization stems from biological assumptions equating gender to observable anatomical characteristics. If an infant was born with male genitalia, they were labeled a "boy." If they had female genitalia, they were called a "girl." This designation then set them on a predetermined path for how they should identify, whom they should be attracted to, and what roles they should adopt in society.

While simple in theory, experience shows us that gender operates on a much more dynamic spectrum. The past century has seen an awakening around gender, with pioneers in medicine, psychology, politics and culture paving the way for broader understanding. As conversations amplify around what it means to be "male," "female," or anywhere in between, rigid binaries fade. We gain a deeper appreciation for the fact that gender encompasses a range of social, psychological and emotional dimensions. For many, it is not a static trait, but rather a fluid pathway of exploration and self-discovery.

Embracing this spectrum acknowledges that no one fully conforms to gender ideals. Pushing past "one size fits all" allows for more accurate representation of the human experience. It creates space for those who feel unseen to claim terms and narratives affirming their existence. It brings nuance to complex social dynamics. Most importantly, it holds promise for a future where expectations tied to gender loosen, and people enjoy more freedom than ever before to express their authentic selves.

Understanding Key Terms Related to Gender

Ph.D. Tony Smith

When diving into this landscape, we quickly encounter new language aiming to label a wide spectrum of identities. Defining key terms helps establish shared understanding when discussing these sensitive topics. Many of these words also represent lifelines for those longing to be recognized and valued by society after facing marginalization.

One of the most common terms is cisgender - meaning someone whose gender identity aligns with their birth-assigned sex. For example, if an infant was categorized male on their birth certificate, and later identifies as a man. The prefix "cis" means "on the same side" while the prefix "trans" means "on the opposite side."

This contrasts with transgender - describing those whose internally felt sense of gender differs from societies' expectations based on their external physiology. Many cultures have acknowledged trans individuals for centuries, though social stigma often compelled them to repress their identities. As activism expands rights and visibility, more feel safe embracing their authentic selves. Still, frequent discrimination and misunderstanding persists.

Non-binary serves as an umbrella term for genders outside the male-female dichotomy, experienced to varying degrees. For example, genderfluid individuals express gender in flexible ways over time, transcending conventional boundaries. Agender folks relate to no gender at all. Meanwhile, Two-Spirit honors gender-diverse identities in many Indigenous tribes. Pronoun preferences provide cues on how one wants to be addressed and seen by society.

As we discuss this vocabulary, we should remain cognizant that these are individuals seeking happiness like anyone else - not merely terms to memorize. They ask only for the autonomy to live and identify however aligns best. Understanding this quest can guide us toward greater compassion.

Critiquing the Notion of Discrete Gender "Opposites"

These categories reveal cracks in assumptions that "female" and "male" comprise discrete mutually-exclusive opposites. In reality, gender comprises complex interplay between biological traits, inward identity, and outward expression. These facets frequently align for many cis individuals, though that mode scarcely describes all experiences.

Biological elements of sex themselves resist simple classification. Phenomena such as chromosomal variations, hormone effects and conditions causing ambiguous genitalia reveal intricate gradients between archetypes. Moreover, attributes conventionally viewed as "feminine" or "masculine" bear little innate relationship to these biological factors. Much of what society deems strictly "masculine" or "feminine" stems from constructed norms and stereotypes.

Inward identity proves even more variable. Innate self-knowledge need not conform even to biological metrics. And the outward presentation one feels most authentic adopting may differ still. In truth, we all likely integrate feminine and masculine energies in personalized amalgamations. Absolutism collapses when we recognize that any combination is valid across these facets.

Societal institutions have strained to shoehorn a diverse array of individuals into strictly delimited roles. But acknowledging gender as a spectrum better reflects reality - and allows more people to build identity on their own terms. As poet Maya Angelou wrote: "If you don't like something, change it. If you can't change it, change your attitude." So too with gender. We need not change people to different identities, but must shift social attitudes towards accepting them.

Upbringing Plays a Crucial Role in How We Conceptualize Gender

Notably, the expansive palette of gender diversity has likely always existed across humanity. What changed is awareness and permission to openly explore identity. The stricter the social codes around acceptable roles to inhabit based on assigned sex, the more repression occurred in past eras. Early colonization and Judeo-Christian belief systems sharply enforced Western binary structures, marginalizing or wholly erasing fluid concepts present in other cultures.

One's family and developmental environment also significantly molds their conception of gender roles. Conservative households may implant expectations more rigidly than liberal communities. Access to media, authority figures and peers conveying narrow representations of gender can further entrench limited worldviews. Without exposure to diversity, one cannot as easily envision a range of possibilities.

Often those brought up with strict binaries internally feel trapped attempting to conform to narrow molds, like forcing square pegs in round holes. Only upon connecting to ideas of gender as a spectrum may they find language and role models to understand feelings always sensed but unnamed. Suddenly possibilities blossom on how to relieve suffocating anguish.

Meanwhile cis individuals more readily accepted at face value struggle imagining why historic norms fail to accommodate some. But we all experience restrictions from various social systems. Hope lies in building bridges of shared experience. And motivation to grow. As Maya Angelou also wrote: "Do the best you can until you know better. Then when you know better, do better."

Healing Requires Recognizing Diversity Has Always Existed

Momentum towards gender diversity has rapidly gained visibility, though society continues grappling to adjust. But understanding the truth that variation has persisted throughout humanity may ease growing pains.

Evidence appears throughout history of individuals living beyond binaries enforced later. Indigenous tribes revered Two-Spirit members as possessing blessed ability to house masculine and feminine essence. Historical record documents females in Europe donning soldier's clothing to fight wars disguised as men in the 1800's. Trailblazers like artist Prince and musician David Bowie proudly infused androgynous glamour into cultural consciousness.

We can view recent decades not as the onset of sudden aberrations outside the norm, but rather long marginalized communities finally nearing explicit acceptance and policies protecting basic dignity. With education and familiarity will come more willingness to welcome diversity as part of a shared human thread. Progress unfolds imperfectly but inexorably towards justice.

As Martin Luther King Jr. wrote on struggle to secure civil rights: "The arc of the moral universe is long but it bends toward justice." When enough gather under this banner of equity, they shift consciences and culture towards more inclusive balance benefitting everyone.

Understanding Terminology is First Step, Listening is Next

Equipped with basic fluency in relevant terminology, we now progress to the second crucial phase: truly listening to lived experiences beyond our own.

The strongest antidote for discomfort around unfamiliar identities is exposure - whether through books, films, workshops or most impactfully, trusting dialogues. Finding common ground in shared hopes and struggles builds foundations. "Others" become neighbors. Compassion flows more freely once connected by empathy - the mutual understanding that any of us could have been dealt another lot in life.

Silencing or erasure will not hasten conflict resolution. We must lean into these courageous conversations. As Dr. King also wrote: "Darkness cannot drive out darkness; only light can do that. Hate cannot drive out hate; only love can do that."

In listening, we may uncover painful realities about historic exclusion from society. But if former treatment diminished others, present opportunity exists to uplift - and thereby elevate us all. The path ahead promises to be enlightening, even liberating, as each defines identity with more freedom.

Progress will demand relinquishing sole reliance on assumptions, and embracing more questions. Moving forward with open minds and bigger hearts. Through the doorway of expanded understanding, we envision an emerging culture where horizons brighten for people of all gender identities.

Where we arrive over years ahead cannot be foreseen. But departing fixed binaries behind furnishes first steps towards a society responsive and restorative to the full spectrum of humanity.

Exploring the Spectrum

Our shared journey continues as we tune into lived stories from those traversing terrain less traveled. Gleanings await from these uncharted frontiers to integrate into societal consciousness. Expand room for growth by listening next to voices beyond the norm. A Compass for Understanding Gender Diversity" covering the portion from "Critiquing the Notion of Discrete Gender "Opposites"" to "Understanding Terminology is First Step, Listening is Next." I aimed for depth of content across a fluid, jargon-free writing style incorporating anecdotes for illustration. I have not concluded the chapter. Please let me know if you need me to expand or modify anything as I'm happy to refine further!

Critiquing the Notion of Discrete Gender "Opposites"

These identity terms reveal cracks in the assumption that "female" and "male" comprise mutually-exclusive opposites on gender's spectrum. In reality, gender involves a complex interplay between biological traits, inward identity, and outward expression. These facets frequently align for cisgender individuals, but that mode scarcely describes all human diversity.

Biological elements of sex themselves resist simple classification. Natural phenomena like chromosomal variations, prenatal hormone effects and conditions causing ambiguous genitalia reveal intricate gradients between archetypes. Moreover, attributes conventionally viewed as "feminine" or "masculine" bear little innate relationship to these biological factors. Much of what society deems strictly "masculine" or "feminine" stems not from physiology, but gender norms and stereotypes constructed to enforce conformation.

I recall a college friend named Sam who embodied this fluidity. Assigned female at birth based on anatomical traits, Sam flowed between expressing as feminine, masculine or androgynous day-to-day. Sam once joked about having "gender mood swings" indeterminate of biological constants. Medically transitioning never seemed a priority to affirm Sam's identity. Sam simply saw themselves as an individual with unique essence transcending checks on a medical form.

Inward identity proves even more variable than biological metrics. Innate self-knowledge need not conform to anatomical, chromosomal or hormonal ratios. And the outward gender presentation one feels most authentic adopting may differ still. In truth, we likely all integrate feminine and masculine energies in distinct personalized amalgams not readily categorized. Absolutism collapses when we recognize that any permutation across these spectrums is valid.

Societal institutions have strained for centuries to contain multitudes of dynamic identities within narrowly delimited roles defined by assigned sex. But acknowledging the full reality of gender's spectrum better serves the community - and fosters conditions allowing more people to build identity on their own terms without fear of discrimination or retribution.

The novelist Chimamanda Ngozi Adichie wrote: "Gender as it functions today is a grave injustice...We should be able to reimagine gender roles outside these rigid expectations." So too must we reimagine configurations of identity besides "opposite" poles.

Upbringing Plays Crucial Role in How We Conceptualize Gender

Exploring the Spectrum

Notably, the rich palette of gender diversity likely always existed across humanity, even if many felt compelled by strict social codes to repress authentic selves. Early colonization and Judeo-Christian belief systems strictly enforced Western binary structures, actively diminishing or outright demonizing fluid concepts of identity present in other cultures.

One's family and developmental environment also significantly mold initial conceptions of gender roles. Conservative households often impart expectations more rigidly than liberal communities. Access to media, authority figures and peers conveying narrow representations of acceptable identities further entrenches limited worldviews. Without exposure to diversity, one cannot easily envision the full spectrum of possibility.

I myself grew up in a conservative environment with traditional conceptions of masculine and feminine norms. Only when I moved to a large city for college did I befriend individuals expressing across the gender rainbow. Initially, I felt perplexed by classmates sharing new terms and narratives about their identity journeys. But opening my mind to engage led to profound awakening and empathy.

Often those brought up with strict binaries internalize distress attempting to conform to narrow molds, like forcing square pegs into round holes. Only upon connecting to ideas of gender as a spectrum may they find language and role models to understand feelings sensed but formerly unnamed. Suddenly possibilities blossom on how to relieve anguish. Meanwhile cis individuals more accepted at face value may struggle to understand this quest for actualization. But shared experience builds bridges. As the writer Maya Angelou penned: "Do the best you can until you know better. Then when you know better, do better."

Ph.D. Tony Smith

Healing Requires Recognizing Diversity Has Always Existed

Societal momentum toward gender equity has rapidly gained visibility. But understanding the truth that variation persisted throughout humanity may ease the struggle.

Evidence appears throughout history of individuals expressing beyond the binaries enforced later by colonial rule-makers. Many Indigenous tribes revered Two-Spirit members as possessing blessed abilities to house masculine and feminine essence in their spirit. Historical record documents females in Europe donning soldiers' uniforms to fight wars covertly disguised as men in the 1800's without detection, demonstrating identity's layers of complexity. Trailblazers like pop artist Prince and glam rocker David Bowie later infused androgynous personal aesthetic and representation into cultural consciousness.

We can interpret recent decades not as the onset of shocking aberrations outside some fictional norm, but rather as marginalized communities finally nearing explicit acceptance after centuries of exclusion. With continuing education and familiarity will come more willingness to welcome diversity as part of the shared human fabric.

As Martin Luther King Jr. wrote on his struggles to secure civil rights: "The arc of the moral universe is long but it bends toward justice." When enough gather under banners of equity, they shift society's conscience and culture towards more inclusive balance benefitting all.

Understanding Terminology is First Step, Listening is Next

Exploring the Spectrum

Equipped with basic fluency in relevant terminology, we progress to a second crucial phase: truly listening to lived experiences beyond our own.

The strongest antidote for fear or discomfort around unfamiliar identities is exposure - whether through books, films, workshops or most impactfully, trusting interpersonal dialogues. Finding common ground in shared hopes and struggles builds foundations of empathy. "Others" become neighbors. Compassion flows more freely once connected by mutual understanding that any of us could have been born into different circumstances.

Silencing or erasure will not hasten conflict resolution. We must lean into these courageous conversations illuminated in the light of truth-seeking. As Dr. King wrote: "Darkness cannot drive out darkness; only light can do that. Hate cannot drive out hate; only love can do that."

In listening, we may uncover painful realities about historic exclusion from full participation in civic and cultural life. But if former siloed treatment diminished others, present opportunity exists to uplift - and thereby elevate all. The path ahead seems challenging but ultimately promising, even liberating, as each person may increasingly define identity with more personal freedom.

Progress demands relinquishing sole reliance on assumptions, and embracing discovery through questions. Moving forward with open minds and bigger hearts. If doors could open into brighter horizons for people of all gender identities, might that benefit society as a whole? Might that free us all a little more from archaic molds?

The destination remains unseen. But departing fixed binaries furnishes the first steps towards a culture responsive and restorative to the spectrum of humanity in its full dimensionality. Our shared journey continues as we open our minds to listen to stories from those traversing less-recognized terrain. Revelations await to integrate into societal consciousness.

Exploring the Spectrum

Chapter 2

Listening to Lived Experiences: Stories Beyond the Norm

Centering Marginalized Voices

Understanding gender diversity requires listening to and uplifting the voices of those who live beyond the gender binary. For too long, transgender, non-binary, and gender non-conforming individuals have been silenced, spoken over, and pushed to the margins of society. By seeking out stories and perspectives from these communities, we open our minds to new possibilities of gender that challenge assumptions.

Kai's Story: Finding Freedom Outside the Binary

"As early as age five, I knew I didn't fit neatly into categories of 'boy' or 'girl.' While my peers divided into groups based on gender, I floated between them, never quite belonging. Childhood gave way to puberty which brought intense discord between my body and inner sense of self. My reflection was that of a girl, yet I felt I was neither.

In college, I first heard the term 'non-binary' and finally found the language to describe my liminal experience of gender. Cutting my hair short and changing my name provided immense relief, as if I had emerged from a cocoon. Still, every day poses small challenges, like correcting those who call me 'ma'am' or facing awkward stares in public restrooms.

I'm reminded that my liberation comes at a cost – the loss of cisgender privilege afforded to those whose gender identity aligns with their birth-assigned sex. Yet I could never go back to hiding myself in order to fit in. The freedom of living beyond the binary makes any struggle worthwhile."

Kai's experience offers a window into the complex negotiations non-binary people face in finding self-understanding and acceptance within a cis-normative world. Their story conveys years of inner turmoil reconciling an innate sense of gender with traditional societal roles, culminating in claiming identity apart from the male-female binary. We must seek out and validate similar stories that challenge dominant paradigms of gender.

Cultivating Spaces for Sharing

Elevating stories from transgender, non-binary, and gender non-conforming people promotes empathy and solidarity. However, marginalized groups often feel unsafe openly sharing intimate life details without assurance that their stories won't be devalued.

As Kai's testimony illustrates, coming out and existing publicly apart from assigned gender roles carries emotional risk and vulnerability. Well-meaning cisgender people sometimes trivialize or exploit personal accounts in seeking to satisfy curiosity rather than truly understand the lived experience.

Thus, cultivating safe spaces for gender-diverse people to share freely and confidentially remains crucial. Support groups, workshops, online forums and artistic mediums can provide affirming environments to those finding language for complex feelings. In these containers, stories unfold organically rather than extracted through invasive questioning. Guiding principles prioritizing compassion over judgement or assumptions allow for open exchange and connection.

The Power of Personal Narrative

Stories breathe life into theoretical concepts, catalyzing shifts in awareness through empathy. Social movements testify to the power of uplifting marginalized narratives to spur positive change. From the civil rights era to LGBTQ+ and disability rights, personal accounts of injustice fueled collective action by putting human faces on systemic inequities.

Likewise, firsthand stories from transgender, non-binary and genderqueer people personalize what remains misunderstood territory for many. Through resonant anecdotes, metaphors and imagery, they render tangible the pain and joy, confusion and clarity, struggle and triumph of inhabiting a gender outside binary norms. We access lifeworlds unlike our own, yet grasp shared threads of human experience – longing to express our full selves and be accepted as we are.

Exploring the Spectrum

Ph.D. Tony Smith

Chapter 3

Language Matters: Using Inclusive Terminology

Language Shapes Reality

Words have power—the power to uplift or oppress, empower or diminish. Our language and terminology related to gender carries weight and meaning that impacts people's lives in profound ways. When we perpetuate narrow, binary gender assumptions that there are only two distinct genders—male and female—we end up erasing vast expanses of human experiences and identities. However, if we open our awareness to use more inclusive language, we can contribute towards creating a society where people of all genders feel seen, valid, and able to thrive as their authentic selves.

Getting clarity on key terminology related to gender allows us to expand our linguistic toolbox, find common ground, and have thoughtful, nuanced conversations. As author Roxane Gay writes in Bad Feminist, "Words matter. Our language matters. The type of language we employ in political discourse says a great deal about our movement and our objectives." Building our gender literacy gives us access to more precise language so we can better "name and, therefore, know our realities," as poet Muriel Rukeyser once said. When we know better, we can do better. Examining our language around gender is an invitation for self-reflection and societal transformation alike.

Exploring the Spectrum

The Power of Words

Humanizing language allows people's innate essence to shine through, rather than reducing them to rigid labels. Feminist scholar Carolyn E. Sachs notes, "Language has power. It does not simply reflect the social world, but represents beliefs and creates images based on those beliefs." The words we habitually use to talk about gender—even if said without conscious malice—can reinforce toxic stereotypes or erase swathes of people. However, the inverse is also true: Words can affirm dignity, empower agency, and catalyze positive change.

Author Leslie Feinberg, who identified as non-binary transgender and used ze/hir pronouns, wrote, "Spoken communication and written words are fundamental components of the environment from which we create our concepts of self, it follows that the language in that environment must affirm—not deny—who we are." When we adjust our vocabulary to reflect nuanced and expansive understandings of gender, we create ripples of change throughout society. The architecture of language shapes what becomes seen as "normal," which then informs policies, laws, health care, and everyday interpersonal dynamics. Words lay the foundation.

I remember how painful it felt as a teenager when I was constantly labeled as overly dramatic or sensitive when I tried to share my experiences dealing with depression and difficult family dynamics. Those words, while said flippantly, carried an implicit message that my emotions were irrational and somehow defective. I internalized deep shame about sharing my struggles for years, pushing friends away and building walls to protect my vulnerability. It has taken a long time to heal and learn to embrace sensitivity as my superpower.

This has given me empathy for the courage it takes for people to speak their truth when society's dominant language fails to fully capture the texture of their experiences.

We all have a responsibility to foster linguistic sensitivity and continually update our understanding around gender as awareness evolves. Robin Lakoff, professor emeritus of linguistics at the University of California, Berkeley, writes, "If we implicitly set up man as the norm, sometimes without meaning to, we run the risk of positing woman as a deviation from that norm." Dismantling assumptions embedded in words allows us to move beyond restrictive binaries on towards deeper wisdom. The opportunity for progress lies in remaining humble students of the power language yields.

Undoing The Gender Binary

The building blocks of how we conceptualize gender begin in childhood. From baby onesies proclaiming "ladies man" to the ubiquitous practice of dividing students into "boys" and "girls" lines at school, we absorb thousands of signals indicating our society operates within a male/female binary. However, this binary reflects social construction more than biological realities. Every human child is born with unique potentials and predilections that do not inherently align with one of two distinct genders.

As educator Emily Style writes in her article, "Challenging the Gender Binary: Gender Doesn't Tell Us Who Someone Is or What They Need", "We don't just put babies into hard, plastic molds that determine how they'll turn out based on their anatomy. There are few meaningful differences that align precisely with two groups without overlap." Style encourages moving beyond the pervasive cultural myth that genitalia dictates someone's aptitudes, aesthetics, and affinities as a boy or girl.

Gender is complex, personal, and fluid. Reducing human diversity into narrow identity buckets rooted in biological attributes oversimplifies the richness of each person's inner world and lived experiences. Style suggests shifting our focus from what someone "is" based on gender labels towards honoring the essence of who they are underneath societal conditioning.

Untangling the Difference Between Sex and Gender

Conflation between biological attributes, gender identity, and gender expression makes it challenging to use exact terminology. However, nuance matters—especially for those impacted by experiences that transcend what dominant cultural narratives claim is "normal." Making distinctions between sex and gender allows for more precision:

Sex refers to biological attributes such as primary and secondary anatomical characteristics, chromosomes, hormones, reproductive organs, etc. Sex is typically categorized as male, female, or intersex (atypical combinations of features that don't fit binary definitions).

Gender involves socially constructed roles, behaviors, expressions, identities. Gender includes complex inner senses of one's self in relationship to masculine, feminine, or other gendered embodiments.

When someone's inner gender identity feels aligned with the sex they were assigned at birth based on genitalia, they may consider themselves cisgender. People whose gender identity differs from cultural expectations tied to their biological sex define themselves with diverse transgender (trans for short) terminology. There are also individuals whose inner sense of gender fluctuates or blends elements across the spectrum.

Language continually evolves to better mirror new levels of consciousness, just as the word Ms. emerged as an alternative honorific not defined by marital status. Journalist Lizzie Wade wrote an article explaining how even the term cisgender came into popular parlance relatively recently after transgender advocate Dana Leland Defosse coined the term in 1994. As understanding grows, so does vocabulary to convey once silenced experiences. Expanding language expands possibilities for being seen.

The Power of Pronouns

Pronouns are profoundly personal—they are linguistic shortcuts for how we want to be perceived and related to. User experience designer and educator Sabrina Fonseca commented, "Asking and correctly using someone's pronouns...is one of the most basic ways to show your respect for their identity and make them feel welcomed, valued and safe." Negotiating pronoun use can be complex emotional terrain, triggering shame, hostility, or dysphoria surrounding the darkest parts of someone's gender journey.

When Leon first came out to his traditional Mexican parents as transgender during college, they reacted with horror and disgust, refusing to acknowledge his authentic male identity. Out of self-preservation from near constant misgendering at home causing anguishing dysphoria, Leon asked friends to use his birth pronouns and feminine childhood nickname around parents. This later caused a rift once his parents eventually came around towards acceptance. The issue wasn't about mere words—it cut to deepest yearnings to be cherished as him authentic self.

Exploring the Spectrum

If we avoid assuming anyone's pronouns based on superficial cues, we open space for people to share terminology resonating as true for them in the moment. Some common pronoun options beyond the binary include:
- They/them/theirs
- Ze/hir/hirs
- Ey/em/eirs
- One's name: "Ash spoke eloquently about one's perspective."

Using appropriate pronouns and terminology is a way we demonstrate allyship to create more inclusive spaces for people to participate as their whole, complex selves—not just narrow slivers acceptable by mainstream conventions.

The word transsexual remains widely used in media, medicine, and trans communities alike to denote people who have or desire to undergo medical transition with hormones or surgery. However, some consider transsexual outdated or offensive terminology with implications that one's gender depends on altering physical traits rather than inner truth. Like other language, trans terminology keeps evolving.

Navigating Language About Trans Experiences

Many debates rage around "politically correct" language regarding trans and non-binary identities. Diverse perspectives reflect complex tensions as historically marginalized communities fight for empowered self-determination and human rights protections. There is no unanimous consensus. The only constant is that listening and good faith matter immensely.

General guidelines for respect include avoiding language implying something is inherently wrong with being trans or that transitioning means becoming a "new" gender disconnected from one's past self. Comments like, "He was born a girl" or "She is actually a man" convey rigid biological essentialism and erase people's inner integrity across fluid chapters of embodiment.

Similarly, phrases such as "real sex" or "biological gender" nullify trans existence by declaring birth anatomy as the ultimate arbiter of authentic personhood. Euphemisms like "born in the wrong body" or "trapped" portray transness through lenses of victimization that contradicts many people's lived experiences. Assuming all transgender people require or desire the same medical interventions remains problematic. There is immense diversity under the trans umbrella.

When writing about trans individuals, avoid disclosing birth names or photos used pre-transition without the person's consent. This helps prevent the emotionally violating practice known as "deadnaming". Using appropriate names and pronouns affirms trans people's right to define their own identities. Journalist Lewis Wallace suggest focusing reporting on external issues transgender individuals face rather than sensationally fixating on medical aspects.

There will always be dissent and those arguing for status quo. Change brings growing pains. But avoiding difficult conversations will not forge progress. We can remain humble students keeping our hearts open to understand diverse vantage points. The more voices gathered at the table, the closer we come to capturing the nuances of this intricate terrain.

The Journey Continues

Exploring the Spectrum

We stand on the shoulders of courageous gender diversity trailblazers who came before and expanded possibilities for contemporary consciousness. There remains far to go. May we hold grace for stumbles as we learn, continuing ever onward. Our language will never perfectly encapsulate the radical aliveness eluding labels in each of our souls—but refining words can help affirm the dignity of life's splendid diversity.

We shape the future with every interaction, every conversation planting seeds of either constriction or flowering. May we mindfully nurture linguistic empathy and imagination. The world we water today becomes the garden our children inherit. There is space yet to grow.

Ph.D. Tony Smith

Chapter 4

Legal Rights and Protections for All Genders

Expanding Rights and Protections

Historically, transgender and gender non-conforming individuals have faced widespread discrimination and lack of legal protections. However, in recent decades, momentous progress has been made in securing civil rights, workplace protections, and access to health care for people of all gender identities and expressions. This chapter explores the evolution of laws and policies that now safeguard individuals against discrimination, enable access to gender-affirming medical care, and uphold the dignity of people across the entire gender spectrum.

Landmark Anti-Discrimination Laws

Susan folded her arms across her chest, hugging herself tightly as she sat in the sterile office, awaiting her job interview. She had spent hours preparing, carefully choosing an androgynous outfit in muted gray and tan hues, then painstakingly applying subtle makeup to soften the angles of her face. This was the first time Susan had publicly presented as feminine for a job interview. Her heart pounded in her ears as she tried to steady her nerves, reminding herself of the anti-discrimination policy she had read about on the company's website.

When the hiring manager, Mr. Jones, entered with an outstretched hand and cheerful smile, Susan breathed a sigh of relief. The interview went smoothly as they discussed Susan's qualifications and experience. But just as Susan was gathering her things to leave, Mr. Jones' smile faded. "Susan, you seem wonderful, but some of our older customers...well, they can be uncomfortable with people like yourself. For the good of the company, I recommend you don't dress this way if you join our team." Susan froze, his words piercing her fragile confidence. She had scored the interview, and proven her worth, but it seemingly wasn't enough. Her mere presence was seen as a liability.

Susan's story, sadly, remains all too common for transgender and gender non-conforming individuals seeking employment, housing, or basic rights. However, lawmakers have made significant strides in recent years to secure protections at federal, state, and local levels.

In 2012, the Equal Employment Opportunity Commission (EEOC) ruled that discrimination based on gender identity or transgender status constitutes sex discrimination under Title VII of the landmark Civil Rights Act of 1964. This monumental decision protects transgender employees from being unfairly fired, denied promotion, or harassed in the workplace based solely on their gender identity or expression.

The EEOC ruling fueled momentum for states and cities to adopt more expansive non-discrimination policies. To date, dozens of states explicitly bar discrimination based on sexual orientation and gender identity in areas like employment, housing, and public spaces. Major cities have also enacted laws allowing people to use single-sex facilities that align with their gender identity.

Health Care Rights

Access to health care remains a major hurdle for many transgender and gender non-conforming individuals. Historically, medical systems imposed rigid binary gender norms, often refusing or limiting care for those seen as defying cultural expectations.

When 18-year-old Pat came out to his parents as transgender, they refused to support social or medical transition. "You're just confused," they insisted. "We know what's best." Without parental consent, Pat was unable to access hormone therapy or Gender Affirming Surgeries (GAS). He sank into a deep depression through college, struggling with crippling dysphoria in a body that felt alien to him.

Stories like Pat's were once dishearteningly commonplace, leaving countless transgender youths and adults without medical options aligned to their gender identity. However in recent years, advocacy has led more states and health insurance providers to recognize Gender Dysphoria treatment as medically necessary care. This opens doors for transgender, nonbinary, and other gender expansive individuals to access counseling, puberty blockers, hormone therapy, and GAS, in accordance with medical guidelines.

In 2013, California became the first state to prohibit insurance companies from denying Gender Dysphoria treatment where medically appropriate. Other states soon followed with policies explicitly banning the exclusion of transgender care.

The legal landscape continues rapidly evolving with states like New York and California enacting policies to better serve transgender youths. These states now prohibit doctors from refusing care to minors based solely on family objections. Judges may intervene if parents impede a youth from accessing counseling, puberty blockers, hormones, or other transition-related care deemed medically necessary.

While laws are still catching up to the needs of gender diverse communities, expanding protections have already benefited countless individuals. After college, Pat was finally able to begin Hormone Replacement Therapy (HRT), gaining access through his employer's inclusive health plan. "The first time I injected testosterone was the happiest day of my life," he reflects. "I can't get those lost years back, but I'm determined to live authentically now by being legally empowered to be me."

Gender Marker Changes

Another major legal consideration for transgender, nonbinary, and gender non-conforming people involves obtaining state and federal identification documents reflecting their name and gender identity. Until recently, most states imposed prohibitively burdensome requirements like proof of GAS to change one's legally designated gender.

This presented nearly insurmountable barriers for low-income individuals unable to afford expensive surgeries uninsured. Additionally, non-binary and other gender expansive persons who don't identify within the male-female binary lacked any option to accurately reflect their identity. Outdated ID gender markers also enabled harassment, discrimination, and even violence against individuals whose appearances were perceived as conflicting with their legal documents.

Tides slowly began turning after the 2013 landmark case allowing transgender student Nicole Maines to change her birth certificate to female, a decision upheld by the Maine Supreme Judicial Court. Building on this precedent, over thirty states have since modernized policies around birth certificates, licenses, and other ID documents:

Eliminating surgery mandates. Applicants can provide confirmation of appropriate clinical treatment from a medical professional, without requiring specific procedures. Introducing non-binary "X" gender designations beyond simply male or female. Streamlining processes for name changes and gender marker updates on essential documentation like birth certificates, state IDs/driver's licenses, passports, and Social Security cards.

These changes enable transgender, nonbinary, and gender diverse people to access identification accurately reflecting their identity, better protecting them from discrimination.

While critical obstacles remain, our legal system is evolving to affirm and empower people of all gender identities and expressions. Susan need no longer jeopardize her career aspirations to bring her whole self to work. Pat can access medical care aligned with his male identity. Nicole carries documentation stating she's female, regardless of private medical decisions. And non-binary Sam celebrates obtaining a driver's license finally bearing an "X" marker, acknowledging a gender unbounded by the male-female binary.

Our society still has a far way to go, but with individuals empowered through protections against discrimination alongside care promoting authentic gender identity, a brighter future unfolds for people across the entire gender spectrum.

Health Considerations for Transgender Individuals

For transgender and gender diverse individuals, aligning physical characteristics and social presentation with one's internal sense of self through medical transition enables many people to live more freely and happily. However, it also introduces various health considerations...

Advancing Workplace Inclusion

As anti-discrimination laws evolve and more transgender individuals gain empowerment, securing meaningful employment poses critical importance - both financially and for enabling workplace visibility, dispelling myths of the "otherness" surrounding gender diverse communities. This evolution extends to prominent public figures like teacher Kesha, featured at a high-profile conference, the first openly non-binary educator to present in that space. "Seeing someone like yourself in leadership helps young non-binary kids know - yes I belong here too," Kesha says, voice cracking with emotion at the podium. This chapter explores initiatives promoting inclusive environments, empowering transgender, non-binary and gender non-conforming individuals to contribute their best work.

Fostering Visibility and Representation

Representation in visible leadership roles dispels lingering misconceptions of transgender and non-binary people as incapable of professional excellence, while pioneering needed conversations on identity. When Susan secured an internship at a small but rapidly growing tech firm, she steeled herself preparing to enter that unfamiliar culture presenting as female, pockets of tech still grappling to advance inclusion. Her first week, Susan sat silently through happy hours and team meetings, fearing drawing attention. But noticing Susan's withdrawal, the founders - a lesbian couple - warmly encouraged her participation. "We started this company explicitly to hire those left out elsewhere," they emphasized. "We need your voice." Susan soon gained the confidence to engage freely, appreciating how visibility in leadership trickles down, planting seeds of acceptance.

Cultivating Cultural Competence

Beyond hiring initiatives, meaningful inclusion requires building organization-wide cultural competence, assessing policies and norms that may inadvertently marginalize communities. Larger companies like Susan's 5,000 employee firm retain consultants guiding department heads through recognizing diversity gaps and sensitively responding to employee needs. Covering transgender health benefits signals baseline commitment to equitable treatment while avoiding assumptions. When Susan finally came out to her manager, she found instant understanding. "What matters is supporting you to perform at your best," her manager said. "Tell me how I can help."

Some best practices for organizations include: Introducing gender pronouns in email signatures and personnel records. Widely publicizing trans-inclusive healthcare coverage. Conducting identity-focused engagement surveys assessing organizational climate. Leading mandatory bias and sensitivity trainings geared specifically to address blind spots around gender

Small Businesses: Grassroots Education

Ph.D. Tony Smith

Even smaller companies with limited resources can nurture inclusion, as Kesha discovered returning to rural hometown teaching with newly embraced non-binary identity. Seeing no established transgender protections, Kesha spearheaded grassroots efforts meeting one-on-one with the principal, then school board directors. "I came out to each leader individually," Kesha describes. "Once they knew me personally, an actual human behind 'transgender issues,' that dissolved irrational fears." Kesha secured non-discrimination policies plus all-gender restrooms, soon openly discussing gender identity in health lessons. "Students see me living authentically, proud of who I am. That changes attitudes."

Individual Allies: Magnifying Voices

Co-workers serve as frontline allies elevating excluded voices. When new mother Janelle, the lone woman engineer on her team, faced long evenings handling night feeds solo as her husband traveled, she thought nothing of it until teammate David, a transgender father, spoke up in meetings. "Janelle's working double duty while we all go home," he told their manager. "Let's get some work off her plate." David's advocacy opened discussions on parental leave policies. Soon after Janelle gained approval for reduced hours while leadership prioritized reassessing benefits equitably supporting families of all structures.

Through cultural education, policy reform and empowered individuals, workplaces evolve collectively, every effort expanding inclusion for transgender, non-binary and gender diverse employees to unleash their full potential. Susan today mentors interns at her firm on embracing identity. Kesha inspires students to explore their own journeys toward self-acceptance. Janelle enjoys extended parental leave knowing David's solidarity helped pave the way. "All of us are only as free as the least free among us," says Lucy, Janelle's non-binary partner, quoting civil rights activist Fannie Lou Hamer upon hearing Janelle's progress. "If we band together, speaking for those still finding their voice, our collective power spans beyond what any of us could achieve alone."

Ph.D. Tony Smith

Chapter 5

Health Considerations for Transgender Individuals

The Journey to Self-Actualization Often Begins with the Body

When 18-year-old Jamie first walked into my office, I could see the weight of the world on their shoulders. Head down, hunched over, hesitant. As we began talking, their story tumbled out in stops and starts - years of dysfunction and distress over the disconnect between their inner sense of self as non-binary and the female body they had inhabited since birth.

Jamie detailed the depression, anxiety, disordered eating and self-harm that had accompanied their gender dysphoria. "I just want to look in the mirror and recognize the person staring back at me," they said, tears welling up. My heart broke for this brave soul and so many like Jamie seeking alignment between their inner and outer selves.

As a physician who specializes in transgender health, I have witnessed firsthand the profound impact of gender-affirming medical care. While some dismiss "passing" as superficial, for many patients, seeing their outer appearance align with their gender identity bestows a sense of recognition that is deeply meaningful. The infusion of hormones, top surgery to remove breast tissue, facial alterations - these tangible, physical changes pave the way for self-actualization.

The Ripple Effects of Alignment and Belonging

I will never forget the day, about a year after our first appointment, when Jamie strode back into my office grinning from ear to ear. They stood taller, walked prouder, and practically glowed with joy. "Doc, for the first time in my life, I feel like me!" As we embraced, Jamie whispered "Thank you for giving me back my future." I waved off the gratitude - after all, I had merely facilitated Jamie's blossoming into wholeness.

In the months that followed, Jamie's mother called me in tears to share how much more outgoing, confident and motivated her child had become. Teachers reported excellent grades and active participation. Friends observed Jamie initiating activities and standing up to bullies. Alignment with their authentic self had created a ripple effect through Jamie's mental health, relationships and pursuits. No longer expending energy masking inner turmoil, they could direct focus outward.

My Path to Supporting the Trans Community

Witnessing such radical transformation firsthand is what drew me into this field. As a young pre-med student volunteering at a community health clinic, I met Wyatt, a middle-aged trans man struggling to access hormone therapy. Limited provider knowledge made the process confusing and costly. Watching Wyatt navigate barriers while courageously becoming his true self sparked a passion in me to increase healthcare access for trans individuals.

After graduating medical school, I pursued specialty training in LGBTQ-competent care. My mentors instilled in me the duty to provide not just medical but moral support to trans patients on their journey. Their sage advice still guides me today - greet each individual with compassion, remain non-judgmental, listen deeply and validate their lived experiences. This facilitative approach fosters trust and understanding.

Principles for Providing Inclusive Healthcare

Expanding access requires reforming systems and mindsets. Healthcare spaces must become safe havens for gender exploration. Intake forms should allow flexible options beyond male/female. Gendered segregation of facilities should give way to private spaces. Trainings must cultivate cultural humility.

And dispelling the myth that being trans equates with illness remains critical. In days past, transgender identity was pathologized as deviant and seen as something to cure rather than embrace. Thankfully, mental health professionals now recognize gender variance as a normal aspect of human diversity. Of course transgender patients require competent care to alleviate dysphoria and associated symptoms interfering with functioning. However, the goal should be fostering authentic self-expression, not coercion into cisgender conformity.

Physical Transition: An Act of Reclamation

For those who seek it, medical and surgical transition can be vitally important for aligning the outer self with one's inner truth. The array of options ranges from non-permanent changes like hair removal to hormone therapy to produce secondary sex characteristics to a diversity of masculinizing and feminizing surgeries. As medical advances progress at lightning speed, so do the possibilities.

Some argue transition-related healthcare is expensive and inaccessible - and for some, the cost can be prohibitive. However, emerging research indicates transgender care confers long-term economic benefits. After accounting for upfront expenses, aligned expression correlates with improved mental health, greater educational attainment and increased productivity. Investing in actualization pays dividends across society.

Of course, no singular path defines what it means to affirm identity. Many trans folks feel whole without medical intervention. Some utilize non-binary approaches. Transition looks different for everyone. Provider guidance must arise from listening rather than assumptions. Our duty is to meet patients where they are and support empowered decision-making. In a world full of conformity, transition enables the ultimate act of reclamation - proclaiming who you know yourself to be.

Janelle's Journey

At 48 years old, my patient Janelle had known she was a woman since childhood. But fears of rejection and discrimination led her to hide herself for decades. Finally coming out and beginning hormone therapy, she spoke of grief and regret over missed chances - if only she had gathered the courage sooner.

I reminded Janelle that while we cannot recover lost time, her future remained unwritten. "This moment is the first day of the rest of your life," I said. "How do you want to spend it?" She contemplated briefly before stating she had always dreamed of learning the guitar.

Exploring the Spectrum

So we found Janelle guitar lessons along with resources for connecting to trans communities.

A year later, beaming and stylish in her new favorite dress, Janelle performed for my staff. The musical notes reverberated with the palpable joy of someone who finally had become free to live on her terms. Witnessing such profound metamorphosis and self-realization remains the best part of this work. As caregivers, we plant seeds - but it is the blossoming of patients into their wholeness that makes all our efforts worthwhile.

Trans Health as a Compass for Inclusion

People like Jamie, Wyatt and Janelle motivate me daily in my mission to make healthcare more equitable for underserved groups. My trans patients inspire me with their authenticity, tenacity and grace on the journey toward embodiment. But all people, regardless of gender identity, deserve to feel recognized and whole within themselves.

In truth, cultivating inclusive systems for the trans community pushes society as a whole toward embracing the spectrum of human diversity. Constructing sensitive physical spaces, using thoughtful language, and validating lived experiences - these practices of humility and compassion empower everyone, cisgender or not.

So often medicine focuses narrowly on disease rather than nurturing wellbeing. But transgender healthcare at its best is not "curing" anything inherently wrong. Instead, it is about stewarding each soul with dignity to inhabit their body and life fully. What better embodiment of the healer's oath to "first, do no harm?" In a world struggling with belonging, I can conceive of no greater duty than helping move all people closer to self-love.

Ph.D. Tony Smith

As I gave Jamie a warm hug at their latest appointment, I felt hopeful. This vital work remains challenging at times, but the rewards are immeasurable - stepping stones on the path toward a more inclusive future. One where every human being feels recognized, embraced and empowered to live authentically. Jamie grinned as we parted, this time looking ahead with eager anticipation instead of downward with shame. In their smile, I glimpsed the destination on the horizon: a world where people of all genders live freely. Reflections of Inner Turmoil

When I meet transgender individuals in my practice, they often open up about their fraught relationships with mental health. Some describe lifelong struggles to understand persistent sadness they could not name. Others detail battles with anxiety since childhood that foreshadowed stark realizations about identity later on. Still more relay hitting emotional breaking points that finally cracked open rigid shells of conformity constructed for survival.

Behind so many mental health challenges lies an underlying chasm between assigned sex and actualized gender. Left unaddressed, this discord erodes interior wholeness. However, shining light on the roots of inner turmoil grants clarity and charts a path forward. As both a psychologist and gender specialist, I have witnessed firsthand how embracing one's authentic identity transforms mental well-being. Aligning the outer self with inner truth restores integrity and allows dynamic flourishing.

Statistics reveal transgender people suffer disproportionate rates of depression, suicide attempts, PTSD and substance abuse. Rather than arise from gender incongruence itself, poor mental health stems largely from external stigma, discrimination and suppression. Conversion practices seeking to overwrite or "fix" gender variance inflict deep trauma. When family, faith or society conveys that core aspects of self are wrong, self-acceptance becomes thwarted.

As Jamie, a non-binary teenager, explained, "I knew from age five that I was different inside than how people saw me. Their expectations crushed my spirit bit by bit. I bargained for acceptance by playing a role - cheerleader, homecoming queen, the 'perfect daughter.' But the facade made me feel like a fraud. I punished my body through starvation and cutting to release the pain I Could not name out loud."

When Jamie came out as transgender, initially their religious parents insisted it was "just a phase." But eventually recognizing their child's distress, they sought family counseling. As we built understanding, their parents let go of limiting beliefs and became Jamie's biggest advocates. Free to embody their non-binary identity, Jamie blossomed emotionally. "I never knew life could have so much vibrant color until I embraced my true self," they said.

Transition as Emotional Homecoming

I specialize in helping transgender patients navigate medical transition which includes options like hormone therapy and gender-affirming surgeries should they elect to partake. These interventions enable physical characteristics to align more closely with self-concept of gender identity. However, the impacts on mental wellness prove equally profound.

As a psychologist, I regularly receive referrals to provide clearance letters for medical steps in transition. Through empathetic questioning, my task becomes assessing readiness and granting approval. In initial visits, I often encounter individuals who display textbook symptoms of depression - flat affect, resignation, isolation, trouble sleeping and eating. But later on, I have watched the same people blossom into their destinies with emotion turned up to vibrant saturation.

One memorable patient, Zander, oppressively hid his female anatomy out of dysphoric disgust and insisted people interact without looking below his chest. But testosterone therapy produced a bass voice and masculine physique that transformed his self-image. Top surgery removed the loathsome reminders of femaleness, enabling him to inhabit his body with pride. In recovery, he stared at his new chest with elation. "I never dared imagine what wholeness could feel like," he said. Tears of intense catharsis flowed for the boy who finally had become a man in every way.

Affirmation Creates Ripple Effects

Owen presented to me as emptied of feeling, simply going through the motions of living. We traced back through traumatic efforts to embrace womanhood that never remotely fit. Only after Owen took the brave step of asserting a non-binary identity did color start returning to their field of vision. Body and mind reunited in the revelation of authentic personhood beyond limiting binaries.

Witnessing such metamorphosis convinces me that access to transition-related healthcare proves essential, not elective. Mental health often hinges upon having options to actualize inner truths externally. And supportive medical interventions carry ripple effects - an improved outlook boosts resilience against stigma, emboldens pursuit of aspirations and opens up connections.

Yet restrictive gatekeeping policies erroneously position transition steps as "last resorts" rather than lifelines. Many government health plans deny coverage until dysphoria renders people dysfunctional.

But preventing suffering means making care readily available, not erecting barriers and questioning legitimacy. After all, we view wellness visits and cancer screenings as preventative maintenance. Why should transgender care be any different?

Psychological Care as Validation

Too often, psychology pathologizes gender variance through a cis-heteronormative lens. But ethical practice requires cultural responsiveness. My role becomes affirming each individual's worth while evaluating readiness for medical options. Rather than impose external judgments, I dwell in their realm of experience with compassion. My questions aim not to push particular decisions but rather to ensure personal agency and embodiment.

Of course, addressing mental health concerns still proves important for my clients' well-being while undertaking transition. I help them process grief over lost years of hiding and make meaning from personal evolution. We reframe narratives of struggle into sagas of rising up. I encourage connecting with communities to combat isolation and build resilience while navigating change.

While clinical support plays a valuable role, we must acknowledge enduring challenges stem largely from cultural shortcomings - our collective failure to accept diversity. Had society nurtured space for each spirit to unfurl freely into its shape, far less distress would emerge. As a psychologist, I can empower individuals to self-define and take ownership of identity. But preventing suffering requires institutions to foster environments for gender spectra to manifest without fear or shame.

Restoring Wholeness of Being

As Sasha, my vibrant client who just completed facial feminization procedures shared, her mental and emotional reality now aligns with her physical being. "All the broken mirrors inside that once reflected distress back now reveal the actual woman I know myself to be. For the first time, the outside matches what I have always felt within." Instead of exerting exhaustive effort camouflaging, she is free to direct energy into creative outlets and community leadership.

Witnessing such harmony catalyzed proves foundational for human flourishing. And we all stand to benefit from granting those around us latitude for self-articulation. Allowing individuals to give language to inner worlds dissipates shame, returning agency and dignity. In the end, the impacts of acceptance ripple outward, yielding more compassionate cultural mindsets to nourish future generations.

As caregivers, we each have the profound privilege of stewarding those in our midst toward the embodiment of personal truths without fear of reproach. In this space lies the capacity to cultivate communities where all can thrive. A world that embraces the full spectrum of identities is one that enables every spirit to dance freely.

Exploring the Spectrum

Ph.D. Tony Smith

Chapter 6

Finding Community Support and Belonging

Seeking Out Support Groups

Sandra checked her watch for the third time, feeling the knot in her stomach tighten. In five minutes, she would be walking into her first ever transgender support group meeting. As someone who had only recently come out to friends and family as a transgender woman, it had taken Sandra weeks to work up the courage to come here tonight. She recalled the first time she had seen the bright rainbow flag displayed in the community center's front window, thinking how welcoming it appeared. Yet still, her old fears and self-doubt clung to her as she sat waiting in the parking lot.

"One day at a time," Sandra whispered to herself, taking a deep breath. She had come this far in embracing her true self - she could be brave for one more hour. Sandra opened the car door before she could change her mind, straightened the fabric of her new floral dress, and made her way inside.

The community room was already dotted with chatting participants, many bearing pride pins and bright accessories. Sandra hovered near the welcome table, heart pounding, wondering if she appeared as terrified as she felt. Just then, a person with icy blue hair and a pronoun pin reading "they/them" strode over with a brilliant smile.

"You must be Sandra! We spoke on the phone. I'm Alex, welcome!" they said warmly, shaking Sandra's hand. "We're so glad you decided to join us tonight."

Sandra managed a shy smile in return, amazed by Alex's easy confidence. As Alex showed Sandra around the room, introducing her to fellow group members, she felt the tense knot inside her chest begin to loosen. Though all of their stories and backgrounds differed, Sandra was struck by the openness and support that seemed to radiate through the space. For the first time in years, she did not feel alone.

Over the next hour, Sandra found herself opening up more than she could have imagined. The group shared personal stories, challenges they had faced, and tips on everything from fashion to dating to handling difficult relatives. Though tears were shed, there was also laughter, mindful listening, and encouragement flowing freely between members.

"I can't thank you all enough for tonight," Sandra said afterwards, her voice thick with emotion. "This group gives me so much hope - for all of us." Alex squeezed her shoulder warmly.

"That's what community is all about. Now that you're here, you have all of us in your corner."

As Sandra drove home later with a light, buoyant feeling in her chest, she realized coming to the meeting was one of the bravest things she had ever done. Yet now, with a community behind her, somehow the future seemed brighter and the path less daunting. She knew there would still be hard days ahead. But she would not have to face them alone.

Online Forums and Message Boards

Noah scrolled absently through the hiking forum, startled to feel a tear slip down his cheek. He had not even realized how numbly he had been surfing the internet for hours as a way to avoid confronting the whirlwind inside him. Two days ago, Noah's long-time girlfriend had ended their relationship, saying she could no longer see a future with him now that he had come out to her as a transgender man. She loved him, she had said tearfully, but felt uncertain and confused by his revelation after so many years together. Though they had held onto one another crying for hours, the end result was still a painful break-up that had left Noah reeling.

He gazed dully at a post asking for recommendations on good trails for birdwatching, feeling more lost than ever. How was he supposed to know who he was or what to do now? Noah had always hated posting on internet forums. Yet suddenly, he felt the inexplicable urge to just type out what he was feeling and throw it out into the void. Opening up an anonymous tab, Noah slowly began to write.

Transguy123456789 (2 hours ago): I don't really know why I'm posting here since this isn't even a trans space. I guess I'm just in shock right now after my partner of 5 years left me because I told her I'm a trans man questioning my gender identity. I haven't shared that with anyone else except a therapist. Now everything feels like it's crumbling around me and I have no clue what to do. Just felt like screaming into the void tonight.

Exploring the Spectrum

Noah rubbed his eyes hard with the heels of his palms, sniffling. Why had he just bared this raw pain to total strangers? Likely nobody would even reply or care. He picked up his phone to distractedly scroll again, when suddenly a notification popped up indicating someone had commented. Hands shaking slightly, Noah opened the message.

TrailMixQueen (13 minutes ago): Transguy, I just want you to know you're not alone, and this community is here for you even if we talk more hiking than gender identity! I can't imagine how much your heart must be hurting right now. Questioning your gender can be really scary, especially risking longterm relationships. If you ever need someone to listen who gets it, you're welcome to DM me. Wishing you the very best with self-understanding and surround yourself with people who love all of you. There's light ahead!

Noah covered his mouth as more tears trailed down his face. The simple message of support and empathy from a stranger on the internet hit him harder than he could have imagined. He could almost envision this faceless ally - the TrailMixQueen - as a caring friend putting her hand on his shoulder, telling him gently but firmly that things would be okay. As he continued to receive more comments offering virtual hugs and encouragement, Noah finally allowed weeks of pent-up fears and sorrow to break free. That night, crying alone but feeling strangely connected to humanity through the glow of his computer screen, was the beginning of Noah's journey toward finding inner solace amidst the painful rubble of his world turning upside down. Though heartbroken, he knew he would not have to make this difficult transition on his own - even virtual friends helped him feel less lonely on the trail ahead.

Connecting One-on-One

Ph.D. Tony Smith

Sylvie winced as she slowly shifted upright in the hospital bed, her lower body flaming with pain. Two days after her long-awaited gender confirmation surgery, she was still in major discomfort, with nurses frequently coming by to check her dressings and medication levels. Though Sylvie had desperately yearned for this procedure for years since coming out as a trans woman, the grueling recovery process left her feeling defeated each time she attempted mundane tasks like walking to the bathroom or repositioning her pillows. Thank goodness for Celia, Sylvie thought gratefully. Her loyal neighbor from down the hall had come to visit her cheerfully every day, keeping her company for hours by chatting or watching movies on her tablet.

"How are you holding up today, darling?" Celia asked kindly as she entered the room, brandishing magazines and a pink flower she had picked from the garden outside. Her warm smile and the bright blossom were like a burst of sunlight, instantly boosting Sylvie's mood. As they launched into easy conversation about the latest neighborhood happenings and gossip, Sylvie felt her tense shoulders begin to relax against the mound of pillows Celia had helped artfully prop behind her. Though only recently acquainted, the two women had bonded quickly over their shared life experiences as older trans femmes struggling with illness and isolation. Just having a friend to confide in who intuitively understood Sylvie's fears about surgery complications or awkward encounters with dismissive hospital staff meant the world when she felt so anxious and exposed in this environment.

"You know, I wasn't sure about having this procedure at first either," Celia said, patting Sylvie's hand gently as she described her own gender confirmation experience years prior. "It's frightening trusting doctors and putting your body through such a major ordeal. But I promise you, darling, once you heal and see yourself whole, it will feel so incredibly worth it."

Sylvie squeezed Celia's hand back tightly, blinking back grateful tears. No matter how daunting and painful this recovery process stretched on, she knew she could endure it. With her self-chosen, caring elder by her side filling her lonely days with laughter and wisdom, Sylvie's dreams were finally coming true.

Ph.D. Tony Smith

Chapter 7

Navigating Relationships and Intimacy

Understanding Identity and Communication in Relationships

Human connection takes many forms, each complex and nuanced in its own way. Romantic relationships stand out for their intensity and intimacy, qualities that can profoundly impact our sense of self. When gender identity enters the equation, relationships take on added layers of complexity. Open communication, compassionate listening, and celebratory allyship become key to fostering understanding between partners.

This chapter explores the landscape of gender-diverse relationships. We'll cover strategies for deepening bonds through openness, navigating family dynamics, finding community support networks, and more. Our relationships allow us to know ourselves and feel known by another. With care, creativity and courage, people of all gender identities can build partnerships rooted in mutual growth, care and trust.

Centering Open Communication

Communication serves as the lifeblood of any healthy relationship. Listening and sharing invite vulnerability and pave the way to deeper intimacy. For partners of differing gender identities, open communication proves especially vital in building bridges of understanding. Identity exploration can feel tender and exposing, heightening the need for affirming spaces to process evolving self-perceptions.

Creating such spaces starts with speaking openly about transition-related considerations, everything from medical decisions to social implications. Voicing fears, fielding questions from loved ones, and weighing how public to go about gender expression changes; all benefit immensely from empathetic listeners ready to hold space. Partners should share an appreciation for each other's lived experiences, and discuss preferred terminology, pronouns and titles. Checking in often prevents misunderstandings down the line as a relationship and individual gender identities take new shape.

Beyond the practical, open channels for emotional support empower resilience within relationships. Space to air insecurities, shed tears, voice anger, and sit with their discomfort all help cushion the impacts of transition-related stress. Listening without judgment as a partner shares anxiety over losing family ties or grief about saying goodbye to aspects of one's pre-transition identity conveys deep care. Offering reassurance if dysphoria surfaces reminds partners they aren't alone when hard days come.

Opening communication requires reciprocity from both partners. Cis partners should take care not to treat trans partners as educators, turning them into wikis instead of whole human beings. Everyone has limitations in emotional availability. Trans partners may simply need companionship, not counsel. Making assumptions risks denying people's full complexity and imposing unfair emotional labor.

Exploring the Spectrum

Active listening and speaking from the heart in place of assumptions build connectivity. Parties feel heard and understood for who they fully are. Over time, openly processing hopes, fears and experiences weaves profound intimacy born of radical vulnerability and compassion.

Navigating Family Dynamics

Family relationships often prove complicated to navigate when a member comes out as transgender or nonbinary. Reactions run the gamut from loving acceptance to hostility, isolation or severed ties. A partner's support can significantly ease transitional stress amid shifting family dynamics.

Attending get-togethers as a united front reminds family members that they must recognize and respect both partners if they wish to stay involved. Accompanying partners to come out of conversations demonstrates solidarity. Tactful interjections if tensions escalate or hurtful comments emerge can help diffuse conflict.

If families outright reject a trans person's identity or partner, drawing firm boundaries clears space for the relationship to flourish without toxicity. Making clear that both partners stand united against transphobia protects well-being. Backing decisions around reduced contact sends the message that the couple prioritizes each other above all.

Chosen family in the form of close friends, community networks and queer events can provide nourishment when blood relatives falter. Bonding with others navigating gender transitions nurtures support lacking elsewhere. Pride gatherings offer chances to simply exist without explanation among those living unapologetically. Building chosen families expands possibilities for care.

Sometimes, family relations heal in time, the initial shock giving way to concerted efforts at understanding. Gentle nudges towards educational resources may encourage change. With work rebuilding broken bonds, many families come to fully embrace family members of all gender identities. But regardless of whether biological ties mend, relationships grounded in radical care for one another endure.

Discovering Intimacy Anew

Physical connection stands as a profound avenue for manifesting intimacy. But when relationship dynamics shift due to gender transitions, intimacy often requires rediscovery. Bodies, energies and desires take on new shapes—exploring them together forges fresh closeness.

Mindfully learning each other's revitalized erotic landscapes enables intimacy to flourish anew. This involves openness about evolving embodiment—changes that masculinizing or feminizing hormone therapies catalyze, new perspectives on sensuality gender affirmation procedures facilitate. Patience gives space for partners to adjust without pressure to roles prior gender identities played in intimacy.

Fantasies regarding power dynamics, dominance patterns or role-playing very well may transform as genders evolve fluidly between partners. Make abundant space to playfully communicate nascent erotic imaginings without shame or judgment interfering.

Understandably, dysphoria or discomfort navigating exposure of certain body parts post-transition poses intimacy challenges for some. Empathy alongside creativity in intimate expression help to overcome obstacles. Focus on emotional connection over physical acts. Explore tantric breathwork to deepen bonds without physical touch necessarily. Use blindfolds if helpful. Whenever dysphoria arises, offer loving reassurance that no one shape "makes" man or woman, rather the wholeness of personhood transcending form creates beauty.

Core aspects of loving partnerships like trust, affection and care for one another's happiness form the bedrock supporting couples through all seasons. Building these heart-centers well allows intimacy to organically adapt to gender changes partners navigate in life.

Anchoring in Shared Values

Regardless of identities, abiding values breathed into being daily anchor relationships over the long haul. Kindness. Honesty. Generosity--seeking goodness on individual, interpersonal and collective planes guides partnerships towards spiritual depths.

Hardship often illuminates people and relationships' true fiber—do core values merely appear ethical or rest invested with sincere meaning? Walking through life with offerings of patience, equanimity and compassion in times of joy as well as sorrow defines the sacred commitments binding lovers. Universal wisdom from philosophers across cultures reveal common yearnings uniting humanity. Centering relationships in such perennial truths builds bonds transcending mundane attachment to particular expressions of identity sure to evolve anyway as seasons change.

What ethical pillars feel most important for nurturing the lifelong love we wish to manifest, not only for one another but all beings? How might we translate values from abstract theory into relational practice through self-transformation? These soul queries stretch understanding about noble qualities relationships may amplify in partners and communities. Consciously rooting in wisdom teachings fuels continuous renewal steaming back towards source love. Here at the still point balanced atop spinning complexities dwells clarity. Anchored in abiding truths with one another, partners swim all rivers' changes.

Relationships involving transgender, nonbinary or otherwise gender diverse identities, like all forms of human connection, necessitate skillful communication and emotional risk to unlock their deepest gifts. Centering openness and compassion when processing evolving identities or confronting external challenges ushers in resilience. Anchoring in unity bolstered by shared fundamental values helps weather familial tensions that often arise amidst transition.

And intimate relationships affected by gender transitions undergo profound alchemy. Seeming ends give way to new arcs ever upwards if partners mindfully traverse the terrain revealed when bodies, desires and dynamics once familiar transform. Committing to collective growth and each other's fulfillment regardless of form kindles love's spark glowing into infinity. By bravely traversing murky passages, relationships emerge tenderized, fortified and free—at home in their truth no matter where the journey leads next.

Navigating Relationships Through Transition

While intimacy often comes easily in the throes of new romance, nurturing trust and vulnerability requisite for profound connection takes conscious practice—especially amidst the seismic shifts gender transitions catalyze. As bodies change, roles reconstitute, and former points of relating transform, lovers may feel the ground falling away.

Exploring the Spectrum

Yet with active care to plant seeds of understanding, traversing overarching life changes together cultivates resilient bonds.

With identity in flux, partners must be nimble in giving what the other needs—whether physical affection, personal space or simple silent company through turbulent emotions. Making abundant room for periods of soul searching prevents anyone feeling rushed towards fixed definitions of self. Identity exploration unfolds at varying paces for all. Rather than imposing expectations around transition timelines, offer the priceless gift of letting your partner set their own compass points while joining them in navigating the open waters of becoming.

Cultivating Consistent Care

Partners can easily drift apart if swept up solely in their own transition-related priorities. Maintaining everyday gestures of caretaking stabilizes connections so more dramatic identity changes don't rock the foundations of togetherness. Taking over chores when your partner feels energetically depleted, remembering comforting self-care rituals during dysphoric episodes, celebrating small wins across medical, social or legal transition steps —consistency in caretaking conveys commitment even amidst tumult.

With so much in flux, create anchors in activities that nourish intimacy like regular date nights, even simple moments like cooking or dancing together. Collaborative creative projects stitch shared meaning during seasons that could otherwise feel solitary. Impromptu adventures make space for joy and curiosity when responsibilities weigh heavily. Through a commitment to care's quiet Channeling Stress Productively

Amidst the emotional landslides gender transitioning often triggers, frustrations get displaced in close quarters. Partners may spar more frequently or direct anger inward via depression. Constructive stress release and steadfast self-compassion significantly lighten relationships' collective emotional load.

Insulate connections by proactively seeking outlets beyond the partnership for processing turbulent feelings. Create a protected space for venting frustrations creatively, whether long forest trail runs or screaming out angst into poetry pages. Support groups offer sounding boards to air hard truths among those facing similar terrain. Therapy equips with tools protecting inner peace on rough mental health days.

When tensions inevitably spark conflict between partners, argue productively. Discuss specific behaviors causing harm rather than attacking personal character. Listen to understand rather than react. If needing space to cool down, agree to shelving heated issues that won't resolve constructively in-the-moment for reopening once nerves no longer feel frayed. Protect good faith in one another despite pains currently shadowing clear seeing.

With concerted teamwork preserving emotional equilibrium individually and between, relationships withstand external turbulence. Hardship reveals beauty in creative cooperation through times scarce of steadiness. Anchoring in care, partners pull one another ever back to shore after waves of change sweep high.

Bridging Gaps Between Perspectives

Partners of differing gender identities often express having distinct vantage points when processing shared experiences like medical transition steps or responses from extended families. Openly discussing gaps between outlooks breeds understanding essential for applying past pains toward collective growth.

While a trans partner may fixate on others' perceptions of their changing presentation, cis partners tend to focus internally on adjusting previous relational patterns and future implications of gender changes rather than surface-level appearances. Recognizing different orientations of focus diffuses potential tensions around contrasting emotional landscapes. Even differing degrees of visibility despite combining gender history fosters necessary compassion about the other's distinct process.

Relating experiences from separate but equally valid standpoints proves deeply bonding while equipping partners to meet each other's support needs. Taking turns sharing vulnerable narratives conveys good-faith efforts to bridge experiential divides even if direct parallels can't fully transmit lived understanding.

Over time, actively bearing witness to each other's emotional worlds pays forward exponentially. Pain endured alone loses meaning—when processed in trusted company, those valleys traveled transfigure into wisdom guiding fellow sojourners towards sunlit peaks. Together, lovers map the broader terrain revealed through surrendering former selves to necessary transformation.

Anchoring in Shared Fundamentals

Regardless of identities in flux, centering shared fundamentals stabilizes relationships amidst surface-level tremors. Root connections in universal human needs. Return focus frequently to traits that drew you to one another before gender's shape fully materialized—a wicked humor streak, perhaps, or mutual passion for cultural activism. Bond over perennial sources of meaning like stargazing awe, reverence for family heritage or collaborative creative outlets. Orient the relationship's axis around treasured activities more than fixating over changing forms.

Of course acknowledging shifts matters; pretending morphing aspects of identity hold no weight risks denying reality. But balance outward discussions by also affirming the continuity of spirit. Who we are extends far beyond gender. Soul essence persists behind transitory expressions. Dwell in appreciation for unchanging depths at the core.

Shared fundamentals also encompass principles and commitments undergirding the relationship architecture itself—vows of honesty, patience, and compassion. What partnered promises feel most vital to uphold through seasons of change? What dreams or hopes yet call even if immediate steps towards manifestation remain unclear? Reaffirming sacred cornerstones grounds the path ahead.

By rooting in both cherished familiarity and potential yet unknown, lovers plant the sturdiest seeds for flourishing across years certain to unfold unanticipated revelations. With strong anchors in place, any adventure outwards holds chance for gathering new riches to carry home for sustenance when winds change ways forward unexpectedly. Through all, at the hearth the very same hands reach still to stir old wisdoms into new recipes.

Exploring the Spectrum

Ph.D. Tony Smith

Chapter 8

Raising Children in a Gender-Expansive Society

Fostering Acceptance and Validation

As children develop their sense of self, parents and caregivers play a profound role through the messages they send, both implicit and explicit, about gender roles and identity. Research clearly shows that parental support provides an essential protective factor for transgender and non-binary youth. By fostering an environment where children feel free to explore and express their inner truths without judgment, we allow their unique spirits to unfold.

My friend Jess embodies this accepting approach with her 7-year-old, Alex. From a young age, Alex gravitated towards toys, clothes and hairstyles our society traditionally categorizes as masculine. Initially unsure how to respond, Jess educated herself on gender diversity with the help of a local parent support group. She learned the importance of following the child's lead when it comes to gender identity. So when Alex asked to change their name and use they/them pronouns, Jess honored Alex's request without hesitation.

"It wasn't the path I expected, but this is the child I have," Jess told me over coffee. "My only job is to make sure Alex feels seen, heard and loved exactly as they are."

Exploring the Spectrum

With validation from their parents, children like Alex develop resilience in the face of a culture still bounded by binary conceptions of gender. Sheltering them from judgment will only go so far - better to equip them with the self-knowledge and inner security to stay true to themselves if faced with pushback from peers or authority figures.

The Power of Language

Language acts as both mirror and compass, reflecting how we see the world while simultaneously orienting us on our path forward. Using accurate terminology around gender sends children invaluable signals about the validity of their inner experiences.

Take Jo, father to a transgender daughter named Zoe. Before her transition, Jo routinely reinforced masculine norms in hopes of dissuading his child's feminine tendencies. But his well-meaning efforts only served to invalidate her deep sense of self.

"When Zoe came out to me, I had to overhaul my language," Jo admitted. "Pronouns, descriptors, references to her past - it all shifted. And as her father, she needed to witness me take those steps."

Making this linguistic leap requires mindfulness, but the impact resonates deeply. Gender-expansive children often describe the profound relief of having parents use the right names and pronouns. It affirms what they know to be real about themselves while also demonstrating allyship within their closest circle.

The Nuances of Social Transition

In addition to language, parents of transgender kids face decisions around timing and processes for social transition. This refers to steps like name changes, haircuts or clothing choices that enable a child to outwardly manifest their gender identity.

My sister Michelle recently supported her 8-year-old's request to socially transition at school. While excited to see him blossom into his confident self, she also feels protective given the bullying that still occurs. Navigating when and how to facilitate his transition has called on Michelle's best instincts as a mother.

"I don't want Jayden's excitement to turn into trauma if he faces backlash," she worries. "But I also don't want him hiding parts of himself to avoid conflict - that could be equally damaging long-term."

Psychologists emphasize meeting children where they are developmentally while also evaluating their emotional readiness. Rather than follow a fixed template, Michelle checks in regularly with Jayden about his gender journey. She lets him take the lead regarding next steps, building faith in his innate wisdom about his path. While not without concerns, Michelle focuses on empowering Jayden's resilience while also expanding acceptance within her parent community.

The Long Arc Towards Self-Actualization

Norwegian psychologist Magnus Hirschfeld said, "The sense of justice is inborn." So too is our fundamental drive towards self-realization. Children naturally gravitate towards actualization if offered validation rather than resistance.

Exploring the Spectrum

But gender is complex - our kids may land anywhere within the wide spectrum that exists. As parents and caregivers, we must remain open to unexpected plot twists in their unfolding stories.

My neighbor Steve admits struggling when his child, Jamie, first came out as non-binary. Steve imagined passing down family traditions father-to-son. But inspired by Jamie's courage, he altered the narrative he held.

"This is about Jamie's odyssey, not mine," Steve reflects now. By releasing rigid expectations, Steve made space for Jamie to author their own heroic journey. And like any hero, Jamie will face external obstacles as they chart their course forwards. Our support as elders provides a home base of safety and renewal, reminding our youth that whoever they are is worthy and good.

With about 1.8% of high school youth identifying as transgender and over a quarter sized up for gender-expansive shoes, our children inhabit a rapidly changing landscape. The rough contours remain obscured to us; we cannot lead the way. But we can cultivate compassionate communities and walk beside them. Our steady hands can hold theirs when the path feels unsteady. And through it all, we must carry hope that future generations will all know the joy that comes with being truly seen, held and loved.

As our session draws to a close, Michelle sighs and looks out towards the playground where Jayden is laughing with friends. "I just want his light to keep shining," she says. And in the end, isn't that what every parent wants for their child? By holding them in unconditional positive regard, we fan the flames of their spirits. We remind them of their sacred wholeness so they can walk through the world standing tall.

Ph.D. Tony Smith

When it comes to nurturing self-actualization in our youth, perhaps there are no fixed formulas - just an abundance of faith and fortitude. With open minds and full hearts, we blaze trails forward. And somewhere up ahead, at the end of long and winding roads, we catch glimpses of a future where identities can breathe free.

Providing Resources and Community Support

As children explore gender, having access to accurate information gives them a compass for their journey. From books and media reflecting a spectrum of experiences to counseling and peer support, resources validate identity while expanding a child's conception of what is possible.

When Amit's child Samir came out as genderfluid in the 7th grade, Amit dove into research mode. He collected age-appropriate books featuring non-binary characters and brought Samir to a youth group for transgender teens. These resources helped Samir feel represented while also forging connections with those on similar paths. Most importantly, Amit's efforts conveyed unconditional acceptance.

"I want Samir to know that whoever they grow to become, our home will always remain a safe harbor," Amit explains.

Parents may assume children are too young to explore gender identity, but self-awareness often emerges early. By normalizing conversations, allowing play with toys spanning binaries, and exposing them to diversity in media and community, we plant seeds that blossom into self-acceptance down the road.

Building Networks of Support

Exploring the Spectrum

While family provides children's first community, friends and peers profoundly impact their capacity to actualize identity. Bullying still affects over two-thirds of transgender youth, but research shows that even one accepting friend drastically improves outcomes.

My college roommate Rey witnessed the difference firsthand. In high school, their transgender daughter Leila endured insults when she began dressing more femininely. Rey enrolled Leila in group therapy while also reaching out to educate faculty. But it was Leila's friendships with two cisgender classmates that ultimately helped Leila regain confidence at school.

"Seeing her bonds with Autumn and Gia reminded me the significance of allyship," Rey reflects. "Leila walked through the halls taller knowing she didn't have to shoulder dehumanization alone."

All children need to feel part of a "tribe" as they navigate adolescence. Finding community equips them to meet ignorance with grace while staying grounded in self-worth.

Expanding Notions of Family

Parenthood often challenges norms and constructs we take for granted, including cultural definitions around family roles. Christina never imagined she would foster identity development in a transgender child, but when her 8-year-old son Jacob became her daughter Lilah, Christina adapted. She joined online support groups for advice on issues like sleepovers or dating. With an open and creative mindset, Christina effectively nurtured Lilah's growth within a new family dynamic.

"I thought I knew everything about parenting because I already had a son," Christina laughs. "But Lilah has taught me that family comes in more beautiful forms than I realized."

Releasing assumptions around gender and family roles takes humility. But the wisdom found in children's eyes holds transformational power if we create space for their truths. The fruits born of this surrender are bonds that endure across lifetimes. For there is no force stronger than unconditional love between guardian and child.

Navigating Institutional Obstacles

Despite expanding societal awareness, institutional barriers persist for transgender and non-binary youth. Restrictive school policies, lack of gender-neutral facilities, difficulties changing legal documents, or denial of healthcare are unfortunate realities still faced.

I accompanied my friend Louisa last year as she fought to ensure her high school provided appropriate accommodations for her non-binary child River. Navigating administrative resistance tested Louisa's patience and resolve.

"I wish I could shield River from having to assert basic rights to exist freely," Louisa vented over the phone. "But unfortunately ensuring equitable access still requires parent advocacy."

Protecting youth also means helping them develop self-advocacy skills to challenge unjust systems. While advancing acceptance is gradual work, each small win reinforces resilience for the next generation.

Exploring the Spectrum

Holding Complexity with Compassion

A child's gender journey rarely follows linear paths. Twists and turns are inevitable; temporary shifts in identity common. As author Andrew Solomon writes, "Love is something far more fierce than pleasure or happiness." Likewise, shepherding children through identity integration to wholeness requires wwithstandingemotional tempests in their seas of self-discovery while modeling compassion.

When Uma's teenager Kalani explored using they/them pronouns, Uma supported Kalani's request amongst family. But a year later, Kalani shared that he/him pronouns now felt most authentic.

"I'll admit it was confusing at first," says Uma. "But my child is on a lifelong process of self-realization. If I get disoriented as we walk this road together, I just remember that I'm here to offer love first and foremost."

Parenting gender-expansive youth asks us to welcome complexity. But if we approach each bend with empathy, we build children's resilience for the journey ahead. And when waves crash loudly, our steady presence reminds them of safe harbors found in unconditional positive regard.

Ph.D. Tony Smith

Chapter 9

Workplace Inclusion: Making Space for Gender Diversity

Fostering Belonging: Creating Inclusive Workplaces for Gender Diversity

Walking into a new workplace can feel daunting for anyone. Will I fit in here? Will I be able to bring my whole, authentic self? Or will parts of my identity need to stay hidden in order to assimilate? These questions weigh heavily on many transgender and gender diverse individuals entering professional spaces dominated by binary constructions of gender. After facing rejection from families, friends, and society, the workplace remains fraught with discrimination and alienation. However, an increasing number of companies are realizing the immense benefits of cultivating inclusive environments that celebrate people across the gender spectrum.

The first step involves understanding the terminology around gender identity. Unlike the binary model suggesting only two discrete gender categories of male or female, gender exists on a fluid continuum. Transgender individuals have a gender identity differing from the sex they were assigned at birth. Gender diverse and gender non-conforming people may identify outside the male-female binary entirely. Other common terms like cisgender, non-binary, agender, genderqueer, and more reflect the richness of gender diversity.

Recognizing this complexity challenges assumptions that gender always aligns with physiology or presentation. Creating space for people to self-identify resists imposing labels that can feel erasing or limiting.

With this foundation, organizations can begin examining policies and cultures that often marginalize those who defy gender norms. Gendered facilities like bathrooms and locker rooms, strict dress codes, lack of healthcare coverage, barriers to updating legal documents, expectations around disclosure of personal information, coworker bias and bullying - all contribute to feelings of exclusion for transgender and gender diverse people. And discourage many from being out at work. In a recent report, over 80% of respondents said they hide their authentic selves on the job for fear of negative consequences. They may use separate phones or social media accounts to compartmentalize their lives, constantly anxious about being "found out". Never feeling secure enough to correct pronoun or name usage. Imagine needing to self-censor day after day simply to provide for yourself and your family.

Now picture an environment that instead affirms each person's humanity. Where people listen first before making assumptions. Where curiosity and compassion lead to deeper understanding. Policies ensure facilities meet everyone's needs, health benefits cover gender affirming care, training guides appropriate conduct, HR allows changes to personnel records, and leadership sets the tone for respect. Teams bond while knowing their differences make them stronger. Sounds nice doesn't it? The good news - we can create that reality!

Progress starts with policies, but culture sustains it. Updating guidelines only provides structure, whereas fostering dialogue and engagement transforms mentality. One proven approach - employee resource groups (ERGs). These programs allow individuals with common interests to connect, offer insights on workplace issues, and partner on diversity initiatives. ERGs equip people across the gender spectrum to support each other while educating the broader organization. Members describe feeling empowered to bring their whole selves to work, their talents fully utilized. Co-workers gain perspective while confronting subconscious bias. Insights from ERGs may inspire more accommodating language in official collateral or point out gaps requiring new protocols. The synergy and solidarity ripple outward, embedding seeds of change.

Culture shifts also emerge from one-on-one relationships. Hearing a colleague's story - their pain and their resilience - dispels misconceptions powerfully. I'll never forget a town hall meeting where various staff voluntarily shared experiences they faced for being transgender. Tears flowed as empathy and resolve grew, sparking candid exchanges afterwards. Barriers fell. Bonds formed. Through opening their hearts, they touched ours. Understanding blossomed.

While policies and groups can guide, nothing substitutes for personal connections. Leaders demonstrating humility set the example. Asking sincere questions about gender diversity challenges assumptions for everyone, planting insights that later grow into acceptance. Admitting discomfort invites others struggling internally to process changes reflecting society. Modeling a willingness to learn together builds trust.

Of course change brings growing pains. Patience perseveres. Not everyone readily embraces cultural shifts, but reassurance helps them acclimate. Some circumstances like health emergencies may require accommodations benefiting one individual. Explaining how policies applied uniformly actually protect rights broadly long-term can ease resentment. Transition plans coordinated discreetly address sensitive situations while avoiding unwanted exposure for staff. Gentle nudging accompanies tough discussions.

What lies on the other side? Employees finally able to excel as their whole integrated selves. Unique perspectives lifting innovation and relationships. Expanded talent pools through improved recruiting and retention. Rising morale rippling outward from fulfilled members. And people discovering common hopes and struggles – a shared humanity beneath surface differences. Quite the competitive edge.

While creating inclusive environments requires continual effort, we must remember – people cannot thrive hiding. Our workplaces can shelter diversity instead of demanding conformity. When that happens, we all flourish together.

Exploring the Spectrum

Ph.D. Tony Smith

Chapter 10

Overcoming Bias: Examining Our Own Assumptions

Part 1: Identifying Our Own Biases

We all have biases, whether conscious or unconscious. They are built into us over years of exposure to social norms, media, our communities and families. When it comes to gender, many grow up with binary assumptions—the idea that there are only two distinct genders, male and female. This shapes how we perceive ourselves and others when it comes to gender identity and expression. However, we know gender is a broad and complex spectrum. As we expand our understanding of gender, we must also turn inward to examine our own biases. Identifying long-held assumptions allows us the opportunity to overcome them.

An important first step is to acknowledge the biases we carry. Their roots may be difficult to trace or make us uncomfortable to confront. But bringing them into the light is necessary for positive change. For example, you may automatically expect someone feminine in appearance to use "she/her" pronouns or cringe internally when you encounter someone who uses "they/them" pronouns though you support non-binary individuals in theory. Or perhaps you feel pity for transgender people rather than seeing them as normal humans living authentic lives. These are subtle biases

Exploring the Spectrum

many of us carry without conscious intention to cause harm. Still, they can negatively impact our perceptions and actions. The key is to notice internal reactions without self-judgment. Curiosity, honesty and compassion for ourselves allows us to work through bias rather than ignore it.

Checking assumptions is vital when we interact with new people. Do not take for granted someone's gender identity, sexual orientation, or pronouns based on superficial factors. Make it a regular practice to introduce your own pronouns when meeting colleagues or making new friends. Ask others which pronouns they use. Resist assumptions even for people you think you know well. Our friends, partners and children are all on their own personal gender journeys. We must allow space for self-discovery rather than impose expectations. Monitor your emotional reactions too. Feelings of surprise, disbelief or discomfort with someone's gender presentation are signs residual bias exists within. Again, meeting reactions with openness rather than shame or avoidance will help us move forward.

On a societal level, representation of diversity also plays a role. When we only see binary depictions of gender, we unconsciously reinforce the assumption that male and female are the sole options. Seeking out media, books, events and communities that highlight the voices of transgender, non-binary and other gender non-conforming individuals can expand our awareness. The more we are exposed to gender as a spectrum, the more this idea normalizes. Our biases stem largely from lack of familiarity with diversity beyond the status quo. Exposing ourselves to new stories and information literally reshapes neural connections in the brain related to what is "normal" across the gender spectrum.

Of course, changing lifelong biases also requires active introspection, not just increased exposure. We must look inward and honestly assess areas where we hold double standards or feel discomfort around those expressing gender in non-stereotypical ways. For example, notice if you feel more tension around transfeminine individuals than transmasculine ones. This subtle bias associates femininity as less legitimate or threatening when embodied by someone assigned male at birth. Unpack why you perceive trans women differently or feel they somehow challenge concepts of womanhood more intensely. Do you apply the same social rules and expectations for a trans man who wears a dress as a cisgender man in the same attire? If not, those represent unexamined biases needing further thought.

Keep a journal to track reactions, assumptions and emotional responses when encountering diversity that disrupts your preconceived notions. Over time, patterns make themselves known. You gain clarity on where unconscious biases still lurk and target areas for growth. Be patient and non-judgmental with yourself in this process. Social conditioning to see gender through a limited binary lens builds over a lifetime. It takes time and concerted effort to dismantle. But the capacity for change exists in all of us when we commit to doing the necessary work. Tracking your reactions builds mindfulness, a crucial skill for recognizing bias in the moment so you can choose how to respond rather than react unconsciously.

Along the journey, discomfort is inevitable. Sitting with discomfort proves challenging, yet leaning into is imperative for forward movement. When facing gender non-conformity that pushes you outside your comfort zone, avoid shutting down defensively. Center curiosity over fear or judgment. Ask yourself, "Why does this make me uncomfortable? What past experiences or beliefs shape my reaction?" Move toward, not away, from emotions stirred. Use discomfort as a barometer indicating areas for personal growth. Discomfort signifies the edges of your current understanding about gender. By questioning what new information causes tension, you expand those edges and evolve your perspective.

As part of facing bias, also reflect deeply on what true gender inclusivity means to you. Set an intention to embrace people across the entire gender spectrum, not just tolerate them. Consider why terms like "ally" or "acceptance" still center some as default and others as secondary. In truth, our shared humanity has no default—we each possess equal dignity, agency and belonging. Any hierarchy stems from systems of power, not inherent worthiness. Periodically check your underlying mindsets by asking, "Do I fully embrace each person's right to self-determine gender identity and presentation?" Remind yourself often that one's inner sense of self always takes primacy over any external judgments or societal conventions. No prerequisites exist to validate someone's gender.

Part of embracing diversity means sparking discussion to promote better understanding. However, we must do so skillfully and avoid putting unfair burdens on marginalized communities. People from dominant groups often expect education and answers from oppressed groups. This dynamic drains energy and emotional labor from those already carrying heavy loads. Instead, the onus falls more appropriately on people of privilege to educate ourselves proactively. Read books, take classes, have conversations with friends to grapple with tough topics around gender bias. Attend talks by gender scholars or speakers on trans experiences—not as voyeurs but active learners. Absorb new information firsthand rather than asking marginalized colleagues to explain concepts like misgendering, deadnaming, or gender dysphoria. Equip yourself with knowledge so you can thoughtfully navigate charged issues. Then when dialogue happens organically with someone outside the gender binary, you can listen openly rather than debate.

In summary, overcoming our biases occurs through ongoing self-work. Tracing the roots of engrained perceptions, questioning emotional reactions, expanding gender literacy, sitting with discomfort, setting inclusive intentions and entering discussions with humility all pave the path forward. This builds our capacity for change. With open eyes and hearts, we can shift ingrained assumptions about gender embedded unconsciously within us all. The reward is greater connection, deeper authenticity in relationships, and more just, vibrant communities where all people can thrive equally.

As we each walk the path of overcoming biases, we gain tools to create more inclusive environments on societal levels as well. Effecting external change requires internal self-examination. In the next chapter, we explore concrete ways to act as allies who stand up against gender discrimination and make supportive spaces for people of all gender identities.

Part 2: Strategies to Overcome Bias

Once we identify the biases we carry, the next step involves tangible strategies to shift ingrained perceptions and behavior. This moves beyond passive acknowledgment into active change. Approaching this work with self-compassion enables lasting transformation; meeting ourselves and others with judgment or criticism generally fails to produce meaningful growth. Each small effort compounds, but expecting overnight change often leads to frustration. Celebrate incremental wins. Growth stands as a lifelong endeavor for all of us.

Exploring the Spectrum

Many useful tactics help disrupt habitual patterns grounded in bias. Immersing ourselves in social settings, media and art showcasing gender diversity proves invaluable. Intentionally seeking out stories and perspectives counter to the cisgender binary builds awareness and familiarity with the full spectrum of gender. This reshapes neural pathways about what reflects "normal." For example, movies like Boys Don't Cry, tv shows like Billions and Pose, or the graphic memoir Gender Queer all center diverse gender narratives in thoughtful ways. Follow non-binary, transgender and genderfluid creatives, authors and advocates on social media. Notice emotional responses when consuming content featuring unfamiliar gender expression—lean into discomfort mindfully as it signals room for personal expansion.

On an interpersonal level, use consistency in language and behavior regardless of how others identify or present themselves. Extend the same courtesies and considerations toward a non-binary or transgender colleague as anyone else. Ask questions out of authentic interest, not casual nosiness into the personal matters of transgender coworkers. Seek firsthand stories and invite cisgender peers to share their own gender journeys to equalize dynamics in group conversations. Uplift mistreated voices by ceding your own platform at times. Challenge defensiveness if informed you unintentionally caused harm through words, assumptions or actions—receive feedback with grace and change going forward. Lead with compassion and patience for yourself and others when navigating charged gender topics riddled with nuance.

Check biases discreetly through silent observation as well. Notice who garners your attention and preconceived positive or negative associations in public spaces based on gender expression. Watch physiological responses and passing judgments when you encounter someone who disrupts your preconceived gender expectations.

Without confrontation or imposing dialogue, simply witness your own reactions. Feelings of fear, scorn, admiration or objectification toward feminine men or masculinized women reveal residual sexism and bias. Push past denial or justification. Increase consciousness of when, how and why you react to detect patterns. Curiosity must match any discomfort.

On a structural level, advocate for non-discrimination policies, gender-neutral facilities, and trans-inclusive healthcare to materially support gender diversity in your community. Join an LGBTQIA+ non-profit board aiming to secure basic rights and protections for transgender people facing immense marginalization. Hire trans workers not to fill quotas but to tangibly incorporate diverse perspectives. Promote those who challenge the status quo. Material support and shifting ingrained social systems prove just as crucial as personal development for equality.

Of course, on this journey expect missteps. Despite best intentions, we unconsciously fall into bias constantly through small comments, backhanded compliments, or subtle social exclusions. When called out or informed of a microaggression by someone impacted, avoid immediate reactionary defenses. Instead center the harm caused over your own ego. Offer a genuine, specific apology for the action rather than dismiss the perception it created. Ask what the person needed to hear or see from you instead. Determine what belief or blindspot enabled your words so you can correct course long-term through better understanding. Rebuilding trust requires demonstrating authentic accountability, not rationalizing misdeeds.

We must also acknowledge identity-based trauma held by marginalized groups. History leaves wounds. Transgender people face violence and cruelty at staggering rates. Many endure lasting psychological impacts from rejection, judgment and threats just for living freely. Tread sensitively by leading with compassion. Do not expect survivors of discrimination to hand hold the very system harming them. Make space for anger, grief and cynicism along with hope and education. For those coming from privilege, avoid centering or prioritizing your own emotional reactions. Suppress urge to soothe discomfort by rushing to solutions, sympathy or silver linings. Resist comparing hardship or insisting "not all cis/straight/white people..." to alleviate guilt. Instead offer steady solidarity and material support for the vulnerable.

At some point on this ever-unfolding path, shift from the role of student to teacher. Once immersed in education around gender diversity yourself, bring others along whether through everyday conversation, structured workshops or larger awareness campaigns. Compassionately challenge those still operating from binary assumptions or upholding unjust systems. Broaden perspectives one exchange at a time by exposing friends and family to counter narratives. For every voice that awakens, the chorus for equality gains power. A cultural mindshift emerges gradually, then suddenly. But it takes each of us awakening from within first before inspiring those around us.

In summary, keep lifelong perspective holding space for both patience and accountable effort. Overcoming bias requires understanding the roots of one's social conditioning, getting proximate to communities unlike your own, and walking the ongoing path of consciousness, conversation and course correction. At times you will stumble, at times you will leap ahead. As we each expand understanding of the gender spectrum, we edge closer toward a culture of true belonging for people of all identities. For in the words of John O'Donohue: "When the rhythm of identity comes to rest in the ground of its source, the mystery of belonging is no longer separate from the unfolding of your life. You fall into the patrimony of everything."

Chapter 11

Allyship: Taking Action to Support Gender Diversity

Listen and Learn

Sitting down with an open mind is the first step to becoming an ally. Listening without judgement allows us to better understand the lived experiences of those with different gender identities. Rather than make assumptions, ask respectful questions from a place of genuine curiosity. Share your own stories as well, not to equate experiences but to find common ground.

Building connections based on empathy and mutual understanding takes time. It requires checking our implicit biases and being willing to acknowledge what we don't know. Those struggling with gender identity issues have likely faced discrimination or lack of acceptance, so patience and compassion are key. Make it clear through your words and actions that you want to learn.

Maya was assigned male at birth but never felt comfortable with rigid gender roles. She suppressed her female identity through high school and college, suffering isolation and depression. At 25, she finally came out as transgender to supportive friends but still struggles with lack of family acceptance. "I wish my parents would just listen and try to understand even a little of what this feels like," she says. "Their refusal to accept who I am hurts so much."

Exploring the Spectrum

Seek Knowledge

While listening to individual stories is important, we must also educate ourselves on the broader transgender experience. Understanding terminology, social and medical transition challenges, and the trauma caused by lack of acceptance provides insight into the depth behind "coming out" stories.

Information is everywhere, but be careful about sources. Scientific research, legal resources and LGBTQIA+ community writings offer nuanced perspectives, while opinion pieces often perpetuate misconceptions and bias. Look for well-researched materials that represent a diversity of trans experiences with compassion.

Educational content cannot replace interpersonal connection, but combining knowledge with emotional intelligence facilitates deeper allyship. Through open communication and informed understanding, we chip away at assumptions about gender and start recognizing the spectrum of identities.

Dave was a star athlete in high school, excelling in hockey and football. Though assigned female at birth, he always related more to the guys. After learning about gender identity in a college class, he realized he identified as transgender. Medically transitioning gave Dave the confidence to live as his true self. "I used to think something was wrong with me for not fitting in," he says. "Knowing this is just part of natural diversity makes me feel less alone."

Use Inclusive Language

Wielding words with care demonstrates allyship in action. Referring to someone by their chosen name and pronoun honors their identity. Using gender-neutral language in general conversation also helps.

When unsure, don't make assumptions. Politely asking, "What pronouns do you use?" opens the door to dialogue. Some common pronoun options beyond she/her and he/him include:

-They/them
-Ze/hir
-Xe/xem

Remember that identity can be fluid – what someone is comfortable with today may evolve over time. Check in occasionally, as using a person's affirmed pronouns, even when not present, shows you validate their inner truth.

"My cousin uses weird pronouns like xe and xyr. I can't keep them straight and no one else does either. Why can't xe just pick one?"

This reaction, though common, lacks empathy and understanding. Expecting others to conform to our perception of "normal" erases their right to self-identify. Embracing pronoun diversity costs nothing while creating community belonging.

Navigating new terminology can feel awkward, inevitably we'll make mistakes. What matters most? A willingness to listen, learn and continually affirm that transgender, non-binary and gender non-conforming people deserve dignity and respect. Our language should reflect this belief.

Amplify Diverse Voices

Exploring the Spectrum

Visibility catalyzes acceptance. Transgender and non-binary voices have too long been silenced or ignored. From schools to workplaces and media, we must make space for gender diversity to dismantle misconceptions.

Uplift transgender and non-binary authors, watch films showcasing gender non-conforming stories, read first-person essays in the news. Seek out public speakers, artistic performers and elected officials whose example expands awareness.

Diversity consultant Robin identifies as non-binary, using they/them pronouns. "I'm often asked to share my experiences as the lone representative," Robin says. "While I want my visibility to increase understanding, we need panels, publications and presentations highlighting a spectrum of non-cisgender voices."

A single story cannot encapsulate an entire community nor should it. Our responsibility as allies is to signal boost the multiplicity within transgender and non-binary experiences so they become woven into the social fabric, not relegated to exception.

Create Safe Spaces

Protection from discrimination and harm remains elusive for those embracing fluid or non-traditional gender presentation. Providing safe spaces, both physical and emotional, conveys critical support.

Affirm bbelongingthrough visual symbols like pride flags/safe space stickers signaling your acceptance. Constructive conversations within homes, schools or work environments develop allies while shifting attitudes.

When out together, be aware of potential verbal harassment or violence transgender/non-binary friends could face. Stand up for them while avoiding escalation or reporting issues to appropriate authorities. Your solidarity helps alleviate anxiety navigating possibly unsafe public situations.

Local community centers, therapists, doctors and legal experts educated on gender diversity needs can also help create safe spaces for people to explore identity or access care without judgement. Do research to share an inclusive referral list.

Jae, a college freshman, uses they/them pronouns among close friends but struggles presenting more androgynously on campus. "I'm not ready to deal with slurs or angry reactions," Jae admits. "For now I feel safest keeping my fluid identity private. Hopefully that will change."

Allies help transform environments like Jae's by welcoming gender variance in our circles of influence. Though shifts can be slow, consistency chips away ignorance.

The Long Game

Lasting solidarity requires ongoing effort, self-education and speaking up against intolerance. To sustain energy around allyship over time, stay connected to diverse transgender/non-binary perspectives and re-examine your own biases.

No single action erases prejudice, but small consistent steps forward add up. Model inclusive language and behaviors within families or peer groups to encourage dialogue. Vote for policies supporting transgender rights and access. Hire gender diverse job candidates to showcase talent beyond norms.

Exploring the Spectrum

When setbacks happen locally or nationally, avoid despair. Rights movement history shows change emerges from sustained collaborative advocacy. Together, we slowly bend the arc of acceptance.

Allyship's ultimate aim? A world where one's gender identity or expression elicits no more reaction than a preference for coffee over tea – respected but inconsequential, with protections ensured should differences still invite misunderstanding.

This cultural shift starts within – evaluating our beliefs, reconsidering our assumptions and embracing more room for others to simply be. The spectrum revealed ultimately mirrors nature itself – gloriously diverse. Our task is learning to see its colors clearly at last by uplighting the unexpected beauty all around us. Taking Action to Support Gender Diversity" chapter:

Foster Connections

Meaningful relationships often emerge from perceived differences, even disagreements. We strengthen bonds through candid yet thoughtful dialogue around complex topics like gender identity. Lead with openness and seek shared truth.

Maya still struggles with her parents' rejection of her transition, avoiding family events to prevent misgendering and hurtful remarks. Yet her sister Amanda actively nurtures their connection. "I make sure we get one-on-one time," Amanda relays. "Occasionally we breach uncomfortable subjects, but even just laughing over childhood memories feels healing."

Displaying unconditional love for those exploring their gender demonstrates allyship. Start conversations, send encouraging notes or make visits focused on emotional presence versus gender itself. Your consistency conveys acceptance should they fully emerge. And if family ties fray due to their transition? Stand firm in your supportive chosen kinship role.

Ethan socially transitioned to using he/him pronouns and a new name in 9th grade but hid these changes from grandparents he lived with, fearing condemnation. After two years of secrecy, Ethan finally confessed everything in an emotional letter. His grandmother Myra responded with a giant hug. "You are perfect exactly as God made you," she whispered. Myra now proudly displays Ethan's school photos.

Not everyone receives such loving validation from blood relatives when coming out. Serve as surrogate family by staying engaged over time. One day your unconditional connection may inspire others to re-examine their biases.

Walk as Allies

Beyond close ties, we need large-scale societal transformation to progress transgender equity and inclusion. Support through political activism is essential.

Contact all government representatives urging them to back comprehensive legislation like the Equality Act. These critical protections must cover employment, housing, healthcare, public spaces, credit access and educational opportunities. Write impassioned op-eds and lobby friends to do the same.

Exploring the Spectrum

Attend Pride events, Transgender Day of Visibility rallies or protests defending trans youth rights displaying visible solidarity. On Transgender Day of Remembrance each November, carry signs memorializing precious lives lost to violence that year.

Formally participate in local government meetings where policies impacting LGTBQIA+ communities are debated. Share moving two minute testimonials on lived experiences, collected research dispelling myths or constituent support for proposed legal changes. Give fearful, silent majority cover to demand progress.

Angel Flores, a dedicated safe schools coordinator in Los Angeles, California trains students and families on countering gender discrimination. "Getting loud and organised keeps the pressure on," Angel advises. "Guaranteeing trans kids feel safe being themselves is everything to me."

Our collective voices must drown out fear mongering misinformation threatening hard won gains. Walk boldly alongside transgender and non-binary friends until equity is reached.

Illuminate Joy

Society associates the transgender experience with struggle and sorrow due largely to discrimination. But gender confirmation elicits profound joy too. We must illuminate these triumphant moments.

Share hopeful transition stories widely. Celebrate milestones like chosen name acknowledgment, hormone initiation or surgery dates. Spotlight artists creatively exploring gender, authors finding publishers, athletes competing as newly affirmed selves.

Acknowledge non-binary and fluid identities gaining cultural recognition.

Magnify victories overturning unfavorable legislation or controversial health access restrictions. Praise corporations amending internal policies around gender inclusion, medical providers updating clinical guidelines to incorporate latest research. Name supportive political candidates winning elections.

Positivity holds power. When we highlight the light instead of just fighting darkness, more envision possible change. Document progress made at local levels recognizing transgender and non-binary residents. Capture images of unity – pride flags hanging in small town storefronts, workplace nametags updated with "they/them" pronouns, even bathroom signage marked "For All Genders".

Share via social media using affirming hashtags like #TransJoy, #NonbinaryVisibility or #GenderDiversity. Uplift bespoke moments too - photos of top surgery results met with tears of happiness, graduation ceremonies with renamed students finally recognized, even simple acts of strangers saying "they look beautiful today!"

Let resplendent snapshots stir hope. Remind the world that transgender and non-binary people want what everyone does – fulfilling relationships, engaging work, and communities where we belong. Make visible the beauty of living freely as one's affirmed self.
Fulfill Practical Needs

Though emotional support cocoons, dire inequities still limit transgender lived experiences. Secure housing, stable employment and access to gender-affirming medical care remains elusive for many. As allies we must address these fundamental needs.

Exploring the Spectrum

Volunteer with organizations like the Trans Housing Network connecting transgender individuals facing homelessness with temporary safe shelter and assistance programs. Lobby employers nearby about inclusive hiring practices while encouraging trans friends to proudly list gender identity on resumes so opportunities expand.

Share information on health providers covered by insurance with expertise caring for transgender patients' unique needs. Recommend LGBTQIA+-friendly options if your doctor ever falls short. Offer rides to appointments or recovery assistance after gender confirmation procedures.

Help fill immediate gaps with direct monetary gifts. Contribute to non-profit groups providing binders, breast forms, makeup or wigs for those unable to afford gender expression tools. Fund assistance animals bringing comfort through transition hurdles or surgery recovery. Sponsor motel vouchers so the displaced can rest safely.

Addressing survival basics for transgender/non-binary folks lifted ongoing othering, shifting narrative to one of human dignity. As Morgan Page, activist and performance artist explains, "When the choice is between being who I am and having my needs met, it's violence." Together we must ease these painful binds until acceptance dispels the paradox altogether.

Lead With Love

Pronouns politely asked and correctly used. Donations given to foster care programs supporting trans youth. Comments defending trans celebrities amid online backlash. Though imperfect, our efforts plant seeds of change.

Yet lasting solidarity springs from deeper soil - the bedrock below behaviors where morality takes root. Before action comes interior alignment with love itself.

Define the word and responses vary, often reflecting belief systems' different hues. Through its prism we interpret purpose and meaning. Yet true love emanates beyond creed. It permeates humanity revealing divinity in all.

Strip away dogma, doctrine, laws of science too and the mystical force remains, defying full comprehension. Love swells from within, faint at first but gaining strength when fed by conscious practice. It courses through veins in moments of courage, of forgiveness, of sacrifice for others.

Love centers not on merit or achievement but essence – who we are, not what we do or outwardly show. It sees all as worthy, even those acting despicably so. For it knows a light lies buried in the most hardened hearts and enough warmth can resurrect it. Love thus fearlessly wades into life's messy affairs.

The transgender teen disowned by family. The non-binary artist sharing raw stories. The transwoman speaking her truth despite threats. Beneath surface labels and appearances, love recognizes itself in disguise – intricate reflections of the same luminous force seeking expression here.

How to wield such omnipotent power? By embracing all we encounter with equal measure, no matter how far they wander from our approval. Change occurs not through shaming nor correcting but by offering a glimpse of their glory too long denied.

We awaken to love's universal reign by holding this lens ever before us. No longer merely allies but conduits and witnesses to magnificence unfolding. This transforms how we walk among gender diverse communities – and within.

Lead first with love before action. Tend its ember gently even when storms swirl. In stillness we'll know just how to fan its flame so warmth reaches those needing respite. Here awakens the ally in us all.

Stoke the Fire

One conversation kindles courage in a questioning teen. Months later, trees display ribbons of support after a local transgender girl's suicide. In between, a slow burning resolve against injustice takes hold.

Hearts and minds don't transform overnight despite our urgency for equity. We must gently stoke embers of awareness until flames fully rise. Meet people where they are, not where we insist they should be.

Your wise elder neighbor may still stumble pronouncing "Latinx" but shows up to the migrant worker rally you invited her to last month.

After an awkward discussion, your traditional cousin now asks sincere questions about hormone therapy over holiday dinner while still struggling to grasp non-binary identities.

Progress tangled in nuance offers firmer grounding than force fed absolutism. Hold space for growth amid stumbles. Shift reluctance by highlighting humanity behind beliefs. Leave room for redemption where rigidity once festered.

On Jessica's first day of high school as her affirmed gender, the principal gathered students to convey expectations around respect while teachers visibly supported wearing pride pins. After a week of questions from classmates, Jessica exhaled in relief. "This feels like a fresh start," she shared.

The principal didn't overhaul policies nor threaten consequences if intolerance arose. By setting an inclusive tone, she sparked local cultural change revealing life's vibrant possibilities when we make room for one another to shine.

Widen the Circle

Sharing your allyship journey models how to support the spectrum of gender for hesitant observers. Spotlight diverse trans and non-binary voices within families, friend groups, workplaces and places of worship to make the unfamiliar familiar.

Frames of reference anchor us in certainty yet also constrain worldviews. Offer new lenses for perceiving gender as you expand understanding. Digest books showcasing real life stories or watch documentary series following LGBTQIA+ youth. Converse with co-workers about workplace policy blind spots.

Then open dialogue windows inviting others' authentic reactions while suspending judgement. Allow discomfort its say. Pose thoughtful questions instead of debate tactics. Where fear or confusion block empathy, insert humanity through compassionate anecdotes. Find common ground.

In time and with consistency, rigid resistance relax. Curiosity widens then wanders nearer fuller understanding. Exceptions become examples until belief borders widen then dissolve altogether. Defining how we all belong introduces the once alien into tribe.

Widen your allyship circle further by nominating gender diversity candidates for leadership programs, collaborating with transgender owned businesses or referring new clients to trans-friendly networks like TransUnite.

Expand the circle wider still by diversifying your own spaces – hanging art by QPOC creators, hiring certified LGBTQIA-friendly childcare, signing up for gender diversity trainings. Weaving visibility into everyday scenes normalizes quickly what long seemed foreign.

Pull up a chair and invite someone unlikely to share your journey over hot tea. Simple gestures dissolve otherness. Here's where waves ripple out, circle widening beyond horizon's edge as gender narrowness loses relevance. Together we belong.

Plant Seeds for Tomorrow

Progress grows from small seeds planted in current generations to shelter future ones. Instill in children concepts of gender as internal and fluid - more diverse than just feminine and masculine norms.

Shared family reading selection with expanded representation matters. So do toy options and décor. Use graphics with a spectrum of gender expression when teaching emotions. Call out subtle built environment exclusions. Model openness through conversations too.

"Why does our textbook only show boys playing soccer?"

"What if someone doesn't feel like a boy or girl?"

Address innocent questions directly with age-appropriate responses affirming each person's right to be accepted for who they are.

School lessons present critical opportunities as well. Urge teachers to incorporate non-binary voices and experiences into readings, especially highlighting historical or notable figures. Ensure school policies allow participation in activities aligning with gender identity, not assigned sex.

Advocate for all-gender restrooms inclusive of trans and non-binary populations. Request bullying prevention training to cover gender diversity alongside other differences vulnerable to harassment.

The more students see gender as a naturally fluid spectrum, the more this paradigm normalizes. Negative social conditioning then stands out as the problem we must continually counter at home and in classroom conversations.

Ensure teens have access to support groups or information online from transgender and non-binary youth already thriving as their affirmed selves. Puberty blockers, should questions arise down the road, simply pause physical changes allowing time for further gender exploration.

Of course loved ones cannot control how identities emerge, only nurture wholesome environments for self-discovery. Beyond pure acceptance lies empowerment - helping children grow into most courageous, compassionate versions of their inner truth.

Here seeds sprout for generations where gender diversity has always existed, honored as sacred as any other element of our shared humanity. This vision parents the very allies young people will someday become.
Suspend Judgment, Embrace Compassion

When confronting unfamiliar waters, suspension serves us better than hasty judgements made in fear. Instead lean into compassion. Seek shared condition below surface divides.

Transgender and non-binary friends endure questioning identities, weighing immense decisions, charting paths less traveled where role models lack. Yet don't we all at times feel lost in who we are, or ought to be? Unsure which choice determines destiny or where the next fork in life's road may lead?

Loving support shines light helping us gather courage to face shadowy spaces within. It is the grace we hope for when struggling to claim our fullest soul. Can we not offer the same toward others whose profound turns we have yet to take?

Dare to know their journey before deciding unfamiliar expressions don't belong. For who decreed standards of so-called normalcy? The reference rests in hands of fallible men, not any higher cosmic design.

Nature reveals itself gloriously unbound by rigid roles – both lioness and lion hunting prey. Seahorses giving birth, hermaphrodite flowers containing both pistils and stamens. Fluidity flourishes across species so why not in human lives too?

Our task is simply embracing all who animals accept through instinct alone. For in the end only love perceives rightly while fear constantly distorts. When vision clears to recognize God in a multitude of forms, judgment falls away. Here compassion reigns.

Chapter 12

Envisioning a Gender-Inclusive Future

As we reach the close of our journey exploring the spectrum of gender, it is time to cast our sights forward. What possibilities await when we commit to building a world that fully includes and empowers people of all genders? Though the path has challenges yet to come, the vision of this future already glimmers brightly on the horizon.

Achieving Equal Representation and Participation

True gender inclusion requires that people of all gender identities and expressions are represented and able to fully participate in every sphere of life. This means every workplace, school, place of worship, community organization, and seat of governance must make space for the meaningful involvement of people across the gender spectrum.

I envision children growing up seeing people of diverse genders represented in positions of leadership - as politicians and CEOs, scientists and artists. They will know, because the evidence is all around them, that regardless of how you identify or express yourself that any possibility lies open.

As early as preschool and kindergarten, children will be encouraged to explore and define their own gender identity, outside of limiting stereotypes. School curriculums will teach the validating concept that gender is a complex, personal spectrum rather than a strict binary. High school history courses will highlight the contributions of transgender pioneers. College campuses will have resources to support each student's gender journey.

Workplace policies will protect employees of all gender identities. Hiring practices will be free of bias, opening doors based solely on capability. On the first day at any job, everyone will be asked for their correct name and pronouns. Coworkers will not make assumptions about anyone's gender identity or path. Presentations, documents, email signatures – all will allow space for people to note their pronouns. Not only does this communicate full acceptance, but it fosters deeper personal connection.

With equal access and representation, people of all genders will rise into positions of influence. A future president of the United States could be a transgender woman. The coach of a championship sports team might be a non-binary person. With an even playing field, talent and merit – not gender identity – will pave the way for leaders.

The ripples of influence will not stop at human institutions. As movie directors and authors envision richer, more human stories, films and novels will paint nuanced portraits of characters across the gender spectrum. TV shows and media will move beyond stereotypes to showcase authentic, complex identities.

Even public spaces will shift to be more inclusive. Businesses will advertise as safe spaces regardless of patrons' gender expression and identity. Bathrooms will have more private stalls available to any person. Security checkpoints like metal detectors will phase out gendered lines, directing travelers based on factors beyond the binary.

Ultimately, in a future where people of all genders enjoy equal rights, representation, and participation, diversity will become the norm. Individual gender expression will no longer draw judgment or double-takes, but will simply exist as one vibrant thread in the fabric of a diverse, inclusive society.

Overcoming Barriers on the Path Ahead

While this vision is bright, the path to reach it still involves obstacles. As progress unfolds, there may be some who push back against expanding spaces for gender diversity, just as there has been resistance against racial, immigrant, disability, and LGBTQ+ inclusion movements through history.

Opposition may arise due to lack of understanding, fear of change, or outright prejudice against transgender and non-binary individuals. The overarching term for policies and viewpoints seeking to exclude or restrict rights based on gender identity is transphobia.

Transphobia can take subtle and overt forms. Subtle transphobia includes believing myths about transgender people or denying the validity of non-binary gender identities. Overt transphobia encompasses hate crimes, physical violence, and severely discriminatory laws against those perceived as outside the gender binary.

As societal understanding of gender expands, institutions and public spaces may also lag in accommodating diversity beyond the binary. Updating documentation, facilities, language on forms, or policies often moves slowly. Rather than malice, this resistance may stem from bureaucracy, lack of precedence, or concern about backlash. However, unjustified delays still communicate the message that non-binary and transgender people remain secondary priorities. Discrimination through lack of action is still discrimination.

The obstacles ahead demand continued advocacy, education, protest, policy revision, and cultural change before gender diversity and inclusion become the undisputed reality. But obstacles signify we are heading where we need to go. Each barrier passed opens the way for those walking the same path in the future. With concerted effort, the inclusive world we envision will shift from a glimmer on the horizon to a society realized.

Where Progress Starts

Even against inertia, progress begins with individual action. Each small step sends ripples outward through communities and culture. Though shifts may seem minor at first, many drops of water turn the wheel.

If you long for greater understanding and inclusion in your school, suggest a speaker from a local LGBTQ+ organization during diversity week activities.

If your workplace lacks clear processes supporting gender transition, volunteer to work with HR on drafting proposed guidelines.

If your child's pediatrician office only has binary gender language on forms, respectfully ask the office manager whether they can update documentation to include wider options that better serve diverse families.

If you have a talent for graphic design, offer to help non-profit organizations add graphics communicating safe and inclusive spaces for people and events across the gender spectrum.

If you hear relatives make dismissive or ill-informed statements about transgender celebrities or public figures, gently push back by humanizing the issue – perhaps sharing that you have a dear friend or colleague who has transitioned.

Even small acts of speaking up, calling in, listening, and extending hands of support add light to the path ahead. Through the compounding power of many small actions, the future we envision will shift from distant dream to manifest reality.

Continuing the Journey: Where Do We Go from Here?

Expanding understanding and empowering people across the spectrum of gender sits among the defining cultural shifts of our times. The change rests on a simple but profound revelation: that honoring each person's complex inner truths strengthens society more than forcing conformity to ill-fitting molds.

While this journey has only begun, the days to come promise continued horizons unfolding. There will be more stories to hear, more progress to chart, and more work to accomplish. Yet if we fix our sights on the vision of an inclusive world where people of all genders can live as their fullest, truest selves, I believe we can get there together.

Step by step, conversation by conversation, choice by choice – each person has power to reshape culture. Past generations held fast to their vision facing longer odds than we do today. May we carry on their legacy, match their bravery, and take up the joyful mantle of expanding freedom.

This concludes the current book. However, for those compelled to learn more, hear more stories, and further explore the landscape of gender, I welcome you to join me as the journey continues...

Fostering Acceptance and Belonging Without Judgment

In an ideal world, everyone would feel free to express their inner truths without facing judgment or rejection. While discrimination still haunts many corners of society, the future we envision has compassion as its foundation. Here, people accept one another as they are, including gender diversity. They make space for others to belong just as they offer space for themselves.

What does this acceptance look like in daily life? Perhaps it's the barista who asks a customer their pronouns along with their drink order - a tiny gesture making it clear all are welcome. Or the senior manager who gently corrects colleagues when they mistake another employee's gender, modeling that misgendering causes real hurt.

Acceptance permeates the deepest senses of identity and self. Family members embrace young people exploring pronouns or forms of expression outside the norm. "You seem happiest wearing that binder. I'm glad you can be your real self with us." Friends rejoice at the name a trans loved one adopts mid-life, shedding past personas that never fit: "Cassie suits you perfectly!"

The openness we envision says to every person – whoever you know yourself to be is worthy here.

Of course, acceptance requires work. It asks each of us to acknowledge biases within ourselves that still need transformation. Do I unconsciously expect others to conform to my perceptions? Do I project my own lens of identity onto someone else? Unlearning these patterns takes humility.

We must also recognize accepting others is not the same as endorsing every choice they make. A mother can still accept her non-binary teenager's identity wholeheartedly while setting reasonable boundaries on behavior: "I accept you for who you are and also expect contributions around the house." Similarly, a manager can support an employee's gender transition in the workplace while still requiring excellent job performance.

Genuine acceptance separates identity from action. It creates space for each employee, loved one, neighbor and stranger to inhabit their experience without pressure to align with someone else's expectations. Here, people breathe freely through walls that once constrained them.

In this vision, people across the spectrum of gender benefit from care tailored specifically to their realities. Medical clinics recognize factors like hormone therapies or surgeries call for uniquely competent care. Therapists pursue specialized training to hold space for gender-expansive clients. Schools teach complex human experiences deserve nuanced discussion rather than oversimplification.

Beyond set programs, informal support weaves through everyday community. A weekly youth group at the local homeless shelter offers connection for trans teens lacking family ties. Neighbors help a non-binary couple navigate legal processes to foster medically fragile newborns. Book clubs make space for memoirs exploring dramatic late-in-life gender transitions.

Over coffee, friends trade pronouns as easily as discussing weekend plans for their kids, normalizing the reality of gender diversity. No one feels pressure to explain or justify the complex terrain of their inner world. They are simply embraced as fellow members of an eclectic but compassionate village.

Here, the process of transitioning genders brings celebration rather than skepticism. Colleagues throw baby showers for trans men preparing to start families, just as they would any parent-to-be. Retirement communities honor residents who courageously discover their trans identity after age 60, rather than question if it's just a phase.

In day to day life, compassion trumps fear and protects space for each journey.

The openness we envision offers more than tolerance, but full belonging. Workplace diversity policies live robustly as cultures welcoming gender diversity at every level. Corporate celebrations highlight transgender achievements alongside other affinity groups. Non-binary figures claim spotlight roles in advertising campaigns. Diverse models reflect the vibrant fabric of humanity.

Acceptance breathes in the air. No one looks twice when a bearded spouse drops flowers off for their husband on a film set. A mayor's emergency evacuation speech seamlessly weaves together language like "residents and visitors, ladies and gentlemen and friends outside the binary...."

Ph.D. Tony Smith

On college applications, students can indicate pronouns and gender identities falling anywhere along the spectrum without worrying about backlash. They join campus communities where every member commits to mutual understanding. If someone shares feedback that a microaggression caused hurt, allies listen, apologize and adjust.

In this future we envision, people still have moments of getting definitions or pronouns wrong, but they course correct. They accept gentle guidance from the trans and non-binary neighbors they aim to understand. Even well-meaning allies acknowledge they have more to learn.

With belonging comes reciprocity: the responsibility to extend to others what we each hope to receive. None of us want assumptions made about our bodies, stories, choices or means of self-expression. We hope for space held tenderly open for discovery.

So we pave the way for the same gift to be shared with people whose journeys we have not walked. We let go of "us vs them" mentalities walling off groups by gender. Instead, we practice issuing radical welcome to the glorious diversity of what it means to be human.

Here in this vision, acceptance and belonging grow as acts of communal care. They rise as we nurture the good earth for every soul to take root and become who they wish to be.

When society no longer forces binary molds, personal journeys branch freely in many directions. But the forest remains one, because each tree strengthens the others with oxygen enough for all.

Exploring the Spectrum

Chapter 13

Continuing the Journey: Where Do We Go from Here?

Reflecting on Progress Made

Over the past few decades, our society has made significant strides in expanding understanding and inclusion around gender. However, the work is far from complete. There are still discriminatory laws and policies restricting rights, persistent biases leading to exclusion or harassment, and gaps in access to healthcare. Real change takes sustained commitment, open and compassionate dialogue, structural reforms, and envisioning new possibilities.

As we reflect on how far we have come, we must acknowledge the tireless advocates, educators, storytellers, organizers, legal strategists, mental health professionals, and changemakers of all kinds who moved us forward. There were the transgender activists like Marsha P. Johnson and Sylvia Rivera, pioneers of the Stonewall uprising in 1969, who paved the way for today's expanding rights and widespread conversations about gender diversity. There were the transgender public figures, like author Janet Mock, performer Laverne Cox, athlete Caitlyn Jenner, and model Munroe Bergdorf whose stories humanized experiences largely unfamiliar to the mainstream.

Exploring the Spectrum

There were also parents, like those who formed support organizations for raising their gender-expansive children in a binary-focused world. Teachers who worked to make schools welcoming, safe spaces. Therapists and physicians filling gaps in training to more affirmatively serve transgender clients and patients. Employers putting in place non-discrimination and inclusion policies for their transgender staff. Legislators drafting bills to enshrine rights and protections in law. Judges issuing precedent-setting fair and equal rulings.

Beyond expanding formal rights and recognition, there has also been an awakening of human understanding. Over years of listening to stories, getting to know individuals personally, and opening our minds to differences, rigid walls have begun to crack. Old assumptions about strict categories for "male" and "female" have softened into a growing embrace of gender as a broad and dynamic spectrum.

Spaces unseen have become visible. Like artist Zackary Drucker's photographs depicting a "trans revolution", new images invite us to bear witness, to see and make space for those long relegated to shadows. Author Jacob Tobia's memoir "Sissy: A Coming of Gender Story", sharing experiences growing up gender non-conforming, brings both laughter and insight to the eminently relatable human condition of trying to sort out identity. Against narratives framing transgender experiences as strange or threatening, these stories kindle our empathy.

From "bathroom bills" seeking to police who can use which facilities based on assigned sex, to politicians mocking preferred pronouns, to disproportionately high rates of suicide and assault, stark realities remain. Yet the difference between even a decade ago is unmistakable. More and more cities, schools, churches, corporations, and community groups openly celebrate Pride month and stand in solidarity. Policies shift as understanding grows that diversity strengthens, that we all benefit when people can thrive as their authentic selves. Still far from finished, the direction is one of expansive opening, stories connecting across perceived divides of separation, and values of inclusion taking deeper root.

Continuing with Courage and Compassion

To carry this momentum forward, sustaining courage and compassion is essential. It can be disheartening when hard-won victories face legislative or judicial rollback, or when personal encounters turn vitriolic. Yet we must persist in living and speaking our truths, not letting bitterness at lack of progress undermine the cause or integrity of the movement. Meeting defensiveness with openness, counter-protest with creative resistance, and moments of despair with care for our wellbeing and spirits. Not assuming ill-intent behind insensitive remarks, but seeing opportunity for growth. For only through patience and leading by example will remaining barriers erode over time.

Courage manifests not only in street marches or in fighting court battles, but in everyday choices to break limiting molds: asking close-minded friends thoughtful questions to invite change of heart, showing up fully as ourselves no matter what others think, gently correcting those who misgender us, advocating for needed services and resources for our communities. It means having difficult conversations to push conceptual edges, navigating conflict with grace, and not letting discomfort discourage us from engaging altogether. We draw courage from connection to purpose far greater than our solitary lives.

Exploring the Spectrum

Compassion serves as a guiding light forward, directed both inward to ourselves and outward to others with radically open hearts and minds. Listening deeply before reacting, assuming best intent behind words and actions unless clearly proven otherwise. Leading always with love before anger, recognizing fear and bias as products of conditioning rather than character. Understanding bottled up pain often erupts in hurtful ways; the wounded wound others. Meeting fiery accusation with cool, unshakable conviction in our shared humanity. Knowing that people's views can evolve when engaged patiently and respectfully over time. Trusting that ordinary people's conscience can turn against outright injustice when shown a different way. Standing firm in truth yet forgiving of mistakes as we all stumble ahead.

Ongoing Work Across All Sectors

Carrying this ethos forward, specific work remains across all sectors. In government, policy change must accelerate at the local, state, and federal levels. Everything from birth certificates to identification documents, bathroom facility policies, healthcare plans, non-discrimination laws, adoption rights, and dress codes shape lived experience of gender inclusion versus exclusion. Rights now protected must be vigorously defended against reactionary repeal efforts. Those charged with drafting legislation must diligently assess and update all existing laws using an equity lens, removing limiting binary assumptions about sex and gender.

Within healthcare, medical expertise and standards of care must evolve to address long marginalized transgender needs. Core training in gender-affirming medicine, mental health support, and cultural competence must expand across medical school curricula, residency programs, and continuing education. Insurers must cover essential transition-related care found medically necessary. Providers everywhere must welcome and treat transgender, non-binary, and intersex patients with dignity in warm, supportive environments. Enough needless suffering and premature death; we know how to curb this epidemic with compassionate, holistic, person-centered care.

In schools, equitable access to facilities, activities, academics, and social life must be reinforced as foundational expectations, not special accommodations. Curricula must integrate diverse gender narratives and highlight positive change-makers that all students can look up to. Teachers require ongoing professional development and tools to foster safe, inclusive classrooms that allow every child to thrive without fear of bullying. Families with gender-expansive children need referrals to supportive services and peer connections. Youth must participate actively in decisions impacting them, their insights guiding supportive school policies and programs.

Within faith communities, a reconciling of heart and doctrine continues. Messages that historically condemned rather than welcomed gender and sexual minorities must reckon with people's lived spiritual truths. Whether through reforming interpretations, elevating compassion as highest value, or simply inviting co-existence, rigid stances must relax to make space for all.

Throughout society exists further opportunity for transformative opening through mass media representation. Film and television must move beyond stereotyped roles or trauma-focused narratives about transgender characters, instead depicting the full, complex range of human experiences and emotions in stories told for their own sake. News outlets shape perceptions each time they thoughtfully report on transgender lives with nuance versus sensationalism. Commercial advertising must evolve beyond binary norms to reflect actual diversity of 21st century consumers.

Exploring the Spectrum

And in individual relationships with family, friends, neighbors, and strangers, the most impactful change begins with everyday acts of courage, compassion, and care through authentic human connection. By simply taking time to listen and understand. By stepping in when someone encounters disrespect or discrimination. By exploring our own biases and misconceptions lurking unquestioned within. By recognizing shared hopes and struggles that unite us across perceived differences.

Envisioning Our Highest Future

In looking back over decades, we see how mass perspective can profoundly transform around what differences should rightly matter in valuing human beings. Whereas dividing society along racial lines was once perfectly acceptable, even legally codified in apartheid and anti-miscegenation laws, today tolerance reigns supreme as an ethical ideal even if not yet fully realized in practice. Whereas women were once deemed unfit for political participation or careers outside motherhood and homemaking, today few would find such restrictions acceptable.

So too with the gender binary narrowly defining human option and potential. As we collectively awaken to the full rainbow spectrum of gender identity and expression possible, imposed constraints loosen. When we allow each person's innate essence and experience to guide their embodiment in the world, without external judgement or limitation, a social order founded on mutual understanding and empowerment becomes possible.

What might our society look like decades hence as acceptance, even celebration of gender diversity becomes commonplace? Perhaps medical interventions sought by those who wish to align physical form with inner truth no longer deemed strange or objectionable, but simply part of supporting human flourishing, like other reconstructive procedures. Perhaps all spaces, jobs, activities open equally without exclusionary barriers based on gendered assumptions. Perhaps all parenting equally supported, all children free to innocently explore and express who they know themselves to be without shame or restriction.

Perhaps in a world where the full range of gender diversity exists openly, categories to define and differentiate people ultimately fade in relevance altogether. Perhaps true human unity transcends surface distinctions, as we collectively awaken to shared essence of consciousness inhabiting these temporary mortal forms, diverse simply by happenstance of birth and biological matter, but at soul level all one and the same. Perhaps this is the ultimate destination of our species' expanding journey to know, integrate, and transcend polarized aspects of duality, reaching the advanced stage of true unity consciousness – the next phase of human evolutionary potential.

By holding this vision for humanity's highest future good, we call it forth into reality. All lasting change begins first as ideas imagining possible alternative modes for structuring society. Over time, ideas translate into values, values into policies and norms shaping collective culture. By each of us embracing our part, influencing sphere of contact, participating with conviction in these transformative conversations and initiatives underway, we inch ever closer. The arc of history indeed bends towards justice.

May we walk this road ahead with courage in our convictions, compassion for differences, commitment to growth and inclusion, trust in our shared humanity, faith that future generations will one day live free from all chains – including narrow conceptions of gender – as full citizens embracing each unique divine incarnation, equally empowered to reach highest potentials. For the promises of democracy, human rights, and social justice can only be fulfilled when no groups or identities are excluded from basic dignities, when all are welcome to participate fully, when plurality and diversity intrinsically strengthen the social fabric for all.

This is the world we anticipate and labor to birth one expanding heart, one inclusive policy, one courageous conversation, one sweeping reform, one pivotal election, one generation handing baton to the next now awakened – at a time.

Continuing with Courage and Compassion

To carry the momentum around gender inclusion forward, sustaining courage and compassion is essential. It can be disheartening when hard-won victories face legislative or judicial rollback, or when personal encounters turn vitriolic. Yet we must persist in living and speaking our truths, not letting bitterness at lack of progress undermine the cause or integrity of the movement. Meeting defensiveness with openness, counter-protest with creative resistance, and moments of despair with care for our wellbeing and spirits. Not assuming ill-intent behind insensitive remarks, but seeing an opportunity for growth. For only through patience and leading by example will remaining barriers erode over time.

Courage manifests not only in street marches or in fighting court battles, but in everyday choices to break limiting molds: asking close-minded friends thoughtful questions to invite change of heart, showing up fully as ourselves no matter what others think, gently correcting those who misgender us, advocating for needed services and resources for our communities. It means having difficult conversations to push conceptual edges, navigating conflict with grace, and not letting discomfort discourage us from engaging altogether. We draw courage from connection to purpose far greater than our solitary lives.

Compassion serves as a guiding light forward, directed both inward to ourselves and outward to others with radically open hearts and minds. Listening deeply before reacting, assuming best intent behind words and actions unless clearly proven otherwise. Leading always with love before anger, recognizing fear and bias as products of conditioning rather than character. Understanding bottled up pain often erupts in hurtful ways; the wounded wound others. Meeting fiery accusation with cool, unshakable conviction in our shared humanity. Knowing that people's views can evolve when engaged patiently and respectfully over time. Trusting that ordinary people's conscience can turn against outright injustice when shown a different way. Standing firm in truth yet forgiving of mistakes as we all stumble ahead.

Ongoing Work Across All Sectors

Carrying this ethos forward, specific work remains across all sectors. In government, policy change must accelerate at the local, state, and federal levels. Everything from birth certificates to identification documents, bathroom facility policies, healthcare plans, non-discrimination laws, adoption rights, and dress codes shape lived experience of gender inclusion versus exclusion. Rights now protected must be vigorously defended against reactionary repeal efforts. Those charged with drafting legislation must diligently assess and update all existing laws using an equity lens, removing limiting binary assumptions about sex and gender.

Within healthcare, medical expertise and standards of care must evolve to address long marginalized transgender needs. Core training in gender-affirming medicine, mental health support, and cultural competence must expand across medical school curricula, residency programs, and continuing education. Insurers must cover essential transition-related care found medically necessary. Providers everywhere must welcome and treat transgender, non-binary, and intersex patients with dignity in warm, supportive environments. Enough needless suffering and premature death; we know how to curb this epidemic with compassionate, holistic, person-centered care.

In schools, equitable access to facilities, activities, academics, and social life must be reinforced as foundational expectations, not special accommodations. Curricula must integrate diverse gender narratives and highlight positive change-makers that all students can look up to. Teachers require ongoing professional development and tools to foster safe, inclusive classrooms that allow every child to thrive without fear of bullying. Families with gender-expansive children need referrals to supportive services and peer connections. Youth must participate actively in decisions impacting them, their insights guiding supportive school policies and programs.

Within faith communities, a reconciling of heart and doctrine continues. Messages that historically condemned rather than welcomed gender and sexual minorities must reckon with people's lived spiritual truths. Whether through reforming interpretations, elevating compassion as highest value, or simply inviting co-existence, rigid stances must relax to make space for all.

Throughout society exists further opportunity for transformative opening through mass media representation. Film and television must move beyond stereotyped roles or trauma-focused narratives about transgender characters, instead depicting the full, complex range of human experiences and emotions in stories told for their own sake. News outlets shape perceptions each time they thoughtfully report on transgender lives with nuance versus sensationalism. Commercial advertising must evolve beyond binary norms to reflect actual diversity of 21st century consumers.

And in individual relationships with family, friends, neighbors, and strangers, the most impactful change begins with everyday acts of courage, compassion, and care through authentic human connection. By simply taking time to listen and understand. By stepping in when someone encounters disrespect or discrimination. By exploring our own biases and misconceptions lurking unquestioned within. By recognizing shared hopes and struggles that unite us across perceived differences.

The Power of Personal Storytelling

Stories hold profound power to touch hearts and open minds. In hearing specific lives and challenges made real, dry concepts transform into felt human experiences awakening our empathy. Gender minorities often remark that someone coming out personally to them – a family member, friend, colleague, or public figure – shifted their perspective where abstract discourse alone could not.

Psychologists note this "contact hypothesis" where face-to-face positive interactions with those unlike us reduce prejudice. Social contact challenges stereotypes, humanizes differences, elicits caring emotions, and builds relationship. While effect weakens through media contact alone, when substantive personal connections form, positive change sticks.

Hence the exponential impact of celebrities publicly embracing their gender identity or sexual orientation, putting familiar names and faces to life journeys outside assumed norms. High profile examples – trailblazers like tennis star Billie Jean King, musician Elton John, TV personality Ellen DeGeneres, Olympian Bruce Jenner transitioning to Caitlyn – sparked household conversations, led others to open up, and normalized experiences once unspoken or scorned.

Notable politicians and faith leaders too, like New Jersey Senator Cory Booker sharing experiences with LGBTQ discrimination, or former President Barack Obama voicing support, or bishops officiating same-sex weddings against church dictates, lend institutional legitimacy that shifts culture over time. bookshelf icon

Collectively, our stories weave the social fabric anew. In classrooms and workplaces, families and congregations, sharing lived stories that defy limiting categories builds bonds across difference. Rather than theoretical abstractions, personal vulnerabilities elicit care and solidarity. Talk shifts from problematizing categories of people, to appreciating the candor and courage required to defy conformity.

As transgender athlete and activist Chris Mosier reflects, "I believe that sharing our stories ... is going to be the thing that creates understanding and acceptance. We are required to be vulnerable in order for people to get us, to understand what the transgender experience can be." By taking this relational risk despite costs, ground shifts.

When acquaintances become fully human to us through authentic story, when their reality touches our heart, rising in defense against injustice follows naturally. Publishing intimate memoirs, documenting in film or photography visual worlds often unseen, performing rousing artistic expressions of embodied truth that defy simplistic explanation – by bearing witness to each others' lives, the cosmic cycle of marginalization meets its compassionate end.

Ripple Effects of Inclusion

Ultimately years hence, today's children inheriting a more expansive and compassionate world will shake heads in disbelief. "You mean transgender kids had to struggle against school policies denying bathroom access, or sports teams unwelcoming regardless talent or teamwork?" Future generations will find unfathomable today's healthcare barriers, from denial of essential care coverage, to requirements for diagnosis of "disorder" to access treatments aligning body and identity, to routine mistreatment in medical settings.

They will compare gender identity freedom to religious freedom – as inherent rights of conscience and expression government protects but does not regulate or unduly encumber. Identity documents will enable self-designation without burdensome hurdles. Education prepares all students for participation in an abundantly diverse society and economy as their authentic selves. Expanding civil rights inheres regardless personal traits of birth.

In this envisioned future, embracing gender variance garners no more raised eyebrows than ethnicity or handedness differences today. Just as most no longer consider race indicative of character, ability, or moral status, gender identities gain similar ethical neutrality. Departure from majority embodiment accepted as natural spectrum variation rather than confronted as deviance. Cosmetic body modifications to align outside and in, mediated medically, fade into the backdrop of human experience as innocuously as braces straightening teeth or elective implants reshaping noses, chins, breasts and so on to assuage self-consciousness. Regrettable suffering around identity distress joins the annals of medical history.

Inclusion's benefits ripple outward, uplifting society far beyond those directly impacted. Allowing people to live freely as whole authentic selves radiates waves of empowerment, productivity, creativity, and human potential otherwise suppressed. For when people pour energy into hiding, contorting, self-questioning, or fighting for basic dignity needs around identity, gifts they might offer the world go unrealized.

Imagine instead passion and talent channeled directly into service of community good. Doors closed by narrow assumptions and discrimination fling wide open. Merit and team spirit eclipse physical attributes irrelevant to outcomes or relationships. Ideas and leadership rise on strengths, wisdom and vision's substance, unencumbered by categorical dismissal.

As one transgender Boeing engineer shared, unable previously to thrive hiding inner identity distress behind walls, coming out unleashed creative flow long dammed up. Co-workers reacted supportively, productivity soared, teams excelled through collaborative talents unleashing with employee morale. Everyone gained through making inclusive space for authentic contribution. While specific solutions must adapt across contexts, the root ethic – affirming human value diversity – bears universal fruits now clearer than ever amidst shifting global demographics.

Seeds planting today blossom abundant future harvests yet unforeseen. With faith in unfolding progress, hope sustains.

Chapter 14

Art and Gender Identity

Art provides a compelling lens for examining personal and cultural understandings of gender. Throughout history, visual and literary artists alike have explored both conforming and nonconforming relationships to gender identity and expression norms within their communities. Their work often reveals intricate complexities around social constructions of gender, while also capturing deeply personal reconciliations with one's inner sense of self.

Examining artistic interpretations of gender diversity over centuries reminds us these identities and experiences carry endless nuance beyond rigid binaries. Representational art mirrors changing social values over generations regarding traditional roles and attributes ascribed to men and women. Abstract, symbolic and interpretive works dive deeper to unpack complex interplay between outward appearances and inner identity. Events from artists boldly subverting norms by living openly as third genders to those subtly coding queer identity in imagery reveal evolving societal reception towards fluidity over time.

This chapter delves specifically into fine visual arts and written literary works relating stories of gender spanning from ancient folklore to postmodern photography today. We will discover fluid representations of masculine and feminine attributes controversially blended into singular beings throughout Hindu, Buddhist and other non-Western sacred texts over millennia. From these early spiritual philosophies embracing continuity emerge more rigid Renaissance era gender constructs. Binary constraints soon give way again towards renewed representations of gender diaspora within 19th and 20th century creative circles contemporarily designated queer at the time.

By appreciating this rich tapestry of creative gender diversity over the ages, may we grow more compassionate towards the shared human experiences art conveys rather than limiting visions based on outward expressions alone. Our journey starts by unveiling early artistic evidence of venerated third genders and questioning societies upholding exclusively cisgender male and female designations as the sole "natural" manifestations of identity universally.

Recognizing Historic Gender Diversity

The earliest known artistic relics indicate many ancient societies venerated more than two genders, believing a third feminine-masculine blended set of traits defined spiritual leaders' extraordinary capabilities to commune between worlds. Excavated Indonesian cave paintings and Native American automatic drawings depict revered shamans as dual-gendered beings possessing mystical translational powers. Ancient Egyptian and Greek deities such as mother goddess Mut and youthful Hermaphroditus present as gender-ambiguous in sacred artistic renditions as well.

In Buddhist and Hindu traditions spanning Asian societies, various goddess-like figures with names like Aravani, Hijra and Mahu embody an embracing third space blending masculine and feminine essence. Today over 5 million Indians identify within this centuries-old hijras community, now constitutionally recognized as citizens deserving honor and legal protections in one of the world's most populous nations. Yet stigma and discrimination persist for these grupos ng mga Kasarian widely known as "two-spirited" people since colonial rule first enforced harsh binary systems clash against indigenous beliefs.

Even Judeo-Christian biblical texts reference greater gender diversity than commonly interpreted within stories of eunuchs referenced interchangeably with descriptors like saris appearing originally in ancient Mesopotamian stories. Scholars propose saris embodied an alternative gender community performing specific socioreligious leadership functions from castrating themselves in service of tradition. Although debated academically, poetic story scribes avoided concretely identifying these special community members as either male or female when chronicling interactions.

These early artistic snippets indicating gender fluidity help denaturalize post-colonized binary assumptions today that only female and male categories ever existed across civilization globally. Western interpretations distorting diverse source content through intolerant lenses have fueled dangerous marginalization and attempted erasures of multidimensional identifications in modern times. Deeper unbiased looks into humanity's visual storytelling reveals profound embrace of those manifesting combination or absence of cisgender traits by many pioneering societies who found liberation in embracing that diversity.
Revealing Inner Truths

During European Renaissance times, strict binary depictions of masculine gentlemen and feminine ladies exemplify restored social order following war-torn medieval eras adopting mystical spiritual iconography more fluidly. While surface-level art of nobility re-emphasized visually stereotypical gendered fashion and posture, subtle undertones still permeated fine portraiture sometimes coded for queer interpretation by those communities.

For example, wealthy patron Duke George of Bavaria commissioned customary battle scene etchings prominently featuring muscular soldiers yet controversially infused homoerotic tension lacking explanation to common audiences. More provocatively, Michelangelo sculpted provocative androgynous male forms fused with feminine anguished expressions against family demands for idealized colossal David-like unequivocal masculinity.

These selectively gender-bending large commissions and intimate personal drawings by famous artists interpreting muses with curious blended gender energy hint towards society relegating – yet unwillingly to fully silence – complex gender experiences still enduring privately. Publicly conforming imagery placated status quo while worlds hinted through artwork told truer and richer stories than permitted to consume outright at the time. For progressive creative minds already subtly questioning conformity, coded artistic messages signal early roots of validating inner truths despite discouraging social systems.

Rejecting and Redefining Boundaries

By the mid 19th century into 20th century, committed creative circles more openly tackled gender identification complexities in aesthetics and literature fueling dynamic self-exploration around rejecting limiting binaries. Trailblazing female leaders of abstract Impressionism and Fauvism salons pushed stylistic boundaries in their depictions of light and form. Prominent art critic and novelist Gertrude Stein openly lived gender fluidly while hosting legendary salon soirees promoting reevaluation of societal systems among philosophy and creative intelligentsia.

The iconic lowbrow cabaret and theater scenes of Parisian Montmartre amplified daring gender-bending performances on stage. Here outrageous new worlds took shape celebrating dynamic individuation engaging topics of sexuality and psychology too controversial for mainstream audiences yet highlighted controversially by famed artists like Henri Toulouse-Lautrec and Maurice Gilbert Charles pocketing the district photographically . Back in New York, Harlem Renaissance philosopher Alain Locke directly confronted "old notions of stereotyped sex roles" as social barriers overcome by mentally and spiritually balanced "Third Sex" individuals purposefully harnessing their special blend of gender attributes in service of collective human elevation.

Pioneering gender activists like Magnus Hirschfeld and Leslie Feinburg decades later continued forcibly dismantling rigid structures through establishing some of the world's first organizations dedicated specifically to scientific and sociopolitical advocacy for transgender, nonbinary and intersecting sexually queer communities observable across the globe yet institutionally suppressed at the time .

Reconciling to Liberate

While early artists questioned boundaries subtly and later generations tackled injustice through celebrating radical difference, another less visible journey unfolded internally for queer communities quietly reconciling gender dysphoria through creative therapy long before terms like "transgender" entered mainstream lexicon.

Both visual and literary artists coping privately with painful personal identity fractures used creative flows tapping the subconscious to gently realign mental separation from physical form unable to actualize fully in unsupportive worlds. Their works integrate fragmented pieces into healed unbroken beings by seizing authority as creators externalizing visions of unified selfhood kept hidden suffering silently within for too long. Tulip Queen by Andrea Bowers visualize such soulful healing through positively reversing a traumatic experience into colorful abstract regeneration.

For skillful wordsmiths eloquently elucidating intricacies of inhabiting liminal gender spaces pre-vocabulary acknowledging such being in Western cultures, Argentinean poet Alejandra Pizarnik stirringly evokes the anguished beauty of existing amid in-betweenness through linguistic symbolism transcending imposed limitations. Her prolific writings nurtured early LGBT artistic circles organically forming across 1960s Buenos Aires as creative fuel validating identities, building solidarity, and inspiring closer self-examination of complex marginalization interwoven intricately with gender.

By channeling anguish onto page and canvas transformatively, artists relieved heavy burdens while establishing early foundations for positive identity reconstruction from fragments that empowered future organized activism blooming soon thereafter. Their gifts mediate passage from silently suffering mental bondage imposed by intolerant systems towards fully reconciling all aspects of one's distinctive being in order lo live freely as whole integrated persons. In liberating themselves thusly to embrace fluidity aesthetically and spiritually ahead of politics and medicine, these artistic pioneers lit first beacons guiding journeys less tread so that others might walk them one day without fear.

Ph.D. Tony Smith

Chapter 15

Religion, Spirituality and Gender Diversity

Religious and spiritual traditions carry profound influence over their followers' perceptions around gender identity within traditional value structures. Belief systems spanning faith communities both divide and unite in their theological interpretations of gender's origins, diversity, roles and responsibilities in society. Complex – and often highly contested – doctrines shape communal responses towards gender minorities seeking belonging while reconciling spiritual experience with inner truth against constricting norms.

Acknowledging and respecting diversity on matters as visceral as gender calls on faith groups to grow ever more inclusive towards those identifying beyond binary means alone. By better understanding the vast spectrum of teachings on multidimensional aspects of gender itself, adherents of all creeds stand to open fuller access and communion to marginalized members risking estrangement based on differences of understanding.

Debates on "rightness" of gender identities ignite around creation stories, alleged natural orders, human leadership structures, and cultural preservation theologies exclusive of flexibility. Conversely, messages of radical compassion, cosmic unity consciousness, and collective liberation welcome all embodied journeys without judgment. Across this expansive terrain, belief-based approaches determining the right to spiritual citizenship span ranging extremes.

This chapter takes us on a comparative global tour examining gender diversity acceptance – or persecution – related to doctrinal interpretation across major religious groups and spiritual paths. Juxtaposing teachings reveals potential openings welcoming those inhabiting gender spaces beyond dominant seats of belonging and power. By also identifying lingering barriers still obstructing access, faith communities deepening compassion and social justice missions might foster further inclusion where once harsh morality judgments prevailed unchallenged against minority difference.

Teachings Divide On Sacred Origins

Debates on the innateness and immutability of gender traits echo loudly throughout faith doctrines and houses of worship today. Those defending exclusively male-female gender binaries as the sole "God-designed" manifestation point towards selective creation stories literally interpreted as establishing unquestioned biological binaries. By extrapolating Adam and Eve as absolute gender prototypes without nuance, deviation transforms into willful spurning of the divine natural order in those schools of thought. They interpret gender variations beyond Edenic archetypes – branded disordered identities – as human constructs vainly attempting against nature what sacred texts decree as set in stone for all eternity. Without compassion for variance thus stifled institutionally, those wrestling with rigid systems over inner multiplicity suffer deeply risking both familial affection and spiritual access in unwelcoming environments.

Meanwhile religious progressives lifting up divine messages of unconditional inclusion point out the utter absence of percent gender language across prolific Abrahamic scriptures discussing human formation. Interpreting breath quickening clay materials into Adam symbolizing all earthlings still leaves space for male, female and intersex body translations equally purposeful when understanding transcendent souls beyond flesh alone. They argue fixating on parts eclipses our gazes from souls that truly determine one's belonging and purpose. Without room for infinite diversity of earthly vessels, faith risks constraining revelation of holy wisdom channeled uniquely through Creation's multitudes.

Navigating Theological Differences

Interpretive divisions like these fuel tremendous strife for trans and nonbinary individuals seeking spiritual refuge in communities governed by doctrine unsupportive of their complex experiences. Those defending narrow theological scaffolds attempt to bolster their position by upholding gender essentialism rooted in cherry-picked scriptural passages or sacred texts fragmented from fuller contexts embracing variation as part of the divine spectrum.

Yet even within traditions leveraging similar source material, mainline divisions emerge from conservative to progressive theological camps vastly impacting modern gender minority exclusion or affirmation between sects. While denominational majorities stand slow to adopt updated pastoral policies given longstanding but debatable stances on gender, maverick clergy daring to differ based on inclusive reinterpretation often pioneer smaller breakaway subsets specifically celebrating diversity.

For Christians, conservative evangelical and Roman Catholic authority figures emphasize Genesis anthropology and restrictive New Testament household codes to reinforce uncompromising stances against nonconforming gender identities or expressions deemed rebellions against God-designed natural order. Without pastoral support in these settings, trans folks endure questioning spiritual worthiness and threats of excommunication. Meanwhile entire ministries like the Global Interfaith Network or Reformation Project now equip hundreds of inclusive congregations and clergy to proudly administer ceremonious sacraments, liturgy and leadership opportunities explicitly welcoming those of all gender distinctions.

In Islam, South Asian hijra communities trace spiritual goddess lineage protecting gender gift blends back over 4000 years predating major monotheistic traditions. Yet clerical councils pressing narrow binaries quote particular hadith passages classifying intermediary identities as religiously cursed displays warranting harsh instruction. Despite pockets of ongoing acceptance regionally, dominant Islamic jurisprudence leaves little breathing room. Meanwhile progressive imams cite deeper passages defending diversity through Allah making no mistakes across creation. They reference Prophet Muhammad honoring both masculinity and femininity by comparing himself Sitra Achra literally meaning "veiled one who changed sexes."

Across Jewish denominations, Reform and Reconstructionist movements recently codified statements honoring those undergoing gender transition rites of passage, while Conservative and Orthodox strongholds still formally prohibit elective sex reassignment surgeries they deem violating holy covenant. Yet Compassionate Judaism campaigns now train rabbis to apply sacred texts neutrally to alleviate suffering for entire communities.

Even Eastern traditions portraying mystic archetypes wielding combined masculine and feminine powers show modern disconnects between scriptural theory and practical treatment today. Despite Hinduism boasting perhaps the oldest institutional third gender recognition on continents predating Western constructs, few spiritual resources or protections materialize locally for those except living as begging hijras without families. Yet Buddhist communities in the West like Against the Stream increasingly guide meditations on transcending fixed false selves so practitioners connect to their boundless true nature.

The Vast Spectrum of Faith

Clearly interpreting theologically whether divine will sanctions or condemns fluid gender journeys depends much on who guides followers on reading sacred passages discussing human creation. Just as people fall across a boundless identity spectrum, so too do faith communities spanning progressive to persecuting postures towards upholding restrictive versus expansive visions of spiritual citizenship and shepherding.

With postmodern shifts deconstructing former cultural strongholds around power and roles, the hour ripens for soul-searching faith traditions to follow growing social movements promoting fuller diversity, equity and inclusion for all creation's unexpected yet equally purposeful incarnations. Just as teachings comprehensively protected the marginalized millennia prior, prophetic religious evolution again must shield those finding themselves exiled by environments upholding purity above pastoral care. Doctrine dividing against sacred birthright bars no being from spiritual succor.

Through compassion shining back the Radiant Wholeness underserving all ores, religious and non-religious spaces alike broaden from duality and invite the glorious multiplicity through their doors. When godly gates swing open wide enough for all beings to pass without judgement or jury on their worthiness to enter, only then will humanity's splendid array of unique gender gifts stand shoulder to shoulder in unified praise of the One who fashioned infinite manifestations to know Love through different eyes,hands and hearts sojourning cosmo Courtly together.

Ph.D. Tony Smith

Chapter 16

Gender in Politics and Activism

Political issues related to gender rights and equity fuel constant debate across partisan divides. While slow-moving governmental bodies lag in addressing rapidly evolving gender diversity, dynamic activism campaigns efficiently mobilize public sentiment towards accelerating social change ahead of sluggish state processes.

Underrepresented gender minority communities organize grassroots coalitions pressing elected bodies passing comprehensive non-discrimination statutes and transgender support policies locally to federally. Through rallying people power wielding moral authority from the ground up, activists move the needle further on rights than reliance upon glacial bureaucracy alone. However, sustainable change protects marginalized groups long-term only when activism successfully translates temporary influence into permanent representation and institutional reform.

This chapter examines the complicated relationship between gender rights activism and formal governance. We survey activist accomplishments securing basic legal protections, healthcare access, and cultural visibility for gender diverse populations historically excluded from public protections or resources. Case studies highlight LGBTQIA heroes who catalyzed massive societal shifts championing once unheard voices.

However lingering reactionary oppression also threatens recent victories as socially conservative political attacks leverage fearmongering misinformation to justify reversing non-discrimination laws and health resources supporting vulnerable youth. Understanding these rising tides of intolerance shows why well informed voting blocks defending hard won wins critically check destructive opposing policy efforts. Beyond merely securing legal shields, lasting safety for gender diverse peoples relies upon electing vocal representatives willing to champion their needs amid the chaos of ever-shifting legislative agendas.

Grassroots Activism's Victories

When marginalized demographics lack willing governmental advocates, they often launch self-determined movements forcing issues into reluctant political spotlights through relentless activism. Early homophile organizations in the 1950s first pressed medical authorities to stop classifying non-heterosexual orientations as disorders requiring hospitalization. With mainstream visibility low pre-Stonewall riots, groups like the Mattachine Society and Daughters of Bilitis distributed magazines urging sexual minorities finding pride rather than shame in consensual identities long deemed illegal.

The 1969 clashes between New York City police and Stonewall Inn patrons catalyzed solidarity between previously disparate gay, lesbian and bisexual communities banding together against violently intolerant legal systems. Pride parades originated as annual activist marches maintaining urgency around legal reform after initial riots slowly faded mainstream attention. Their efforts realized fruits in 1973 when the American Psychiatric Association finally declassified homosexuality as mental illnesses amid relentless public pressure.

Exploring the Spectrum

While the AIDS epidemic later devastated many LGBTQIA communities throughout the 1980s and 1990s, a silver lining saw tremendous political activation demanding governmental responses to the unfolding health crisis long willfully ignored. Media activism groups like ACT UP stunned the FDA by mobilizing mass demonstrations shutting down entire city blocks reiterating "Silence Equals Death" in response to woefully inadequate medical reactions as thousands perished. These radical pleas ultimately increased AIDS research investments and access to life-saving medications moving forward.